What people are saying about *The Incredible Four-Year Adventure . . .*

"I heartily wish that this book had been available sixty years ago when I went up to Cambridge University: It would have saved me many blunders! I have known John and Chris Yates from their boyhood, and recently John has been my study assistant for three years in London. So I can testify that what they have written is authentic. It has at least three outstanding qualities: honesty (they don't conceal their struggles), balance (they combine idealism with reality), and wisdom (they draw on their own experiences and their friends' experiences). I warmly commend *Four-Year Adventure* to today's students."
—John Stott, preacher, scholar, and author

"America's Christian youth are our nation's greatest asset and hope. The wonderful, practical wisdom in this book will greatly enhance their transition to college life and prepare them to deal successfully with the exciting challenges ahead."
—Bill Bright, founder and president, Campus Crusade for Christ International

"Every college-bound high school senior has misconceptions about what life on campus will be like. John and Chris Yates expose these stereotypes and the false expectations that derail Christians from living faithfully when they first move away from home. Lordship, integrity, and service form the foundational themes, applied to academics, social life, witness, money, and a host of other life decisions. Parents, pastors, youth workers, and guidance counselors should have this book on the ready. They will get a good clue of how successfully a Christian freshman will navigate the perils and opportunities of college by how seriously the student takes the advice in this book."
—Steve Hayner, president, InterVarsity Christian Fellowship

"This book would be an asset to any student preparing to enter college. John and Chris Yates come fresh from the campus and are able to speak accurately about what an incoming freshman may face."
—Denny Rydberg, president, Young Life

"In Youth for Christ we focus on young people ages 11 to18. But we know from experience that the college years are where a young person's faith is often tested. *The Incredible Four-Year Adventure* will provide practical help in navigating this important time. Buy it for the young person in your life."
—Roger Cross, president, Youth for Christ USA

"John and Chris Yates have hit the nail squarely on the head. This book runs neck-and-neck and shoulder-to-shoulder with Dr. Dobson's *Life on the Edge* as two of the most significant books ever written to the college audience. John and Chris Yates understand the mind and emotions of college students like few who ever lived, with their finger on the pulse of the perilous experience that faces every aspiring high school graduate. These two talented and empathetic authors could save countless college kids from the spiritual and moral failures that so consume high school graduates who grow up in Christian homes but lose their faith and moral integrity during their college years. I see this book as a gigantic lifesaving buoy floating gallantly in a sea of indescribable moral challenges."
—Joe White, president, Kanakuk Kamps

The Incredible Four-Year Adventure

Finding Real Faith, Fun, and Friendship at College

John Yates and Chris Yates

Baker Books
A Division of Baker Book House Co
Grand Rapids, Michigan 49516

© 2000 by John Yates and Chris Yates

Published by Baker Books
a division of Baker Book House Company
P.O. Box 6287, Grand Rapids, MI 49516-6287

Printed in the United States of America

Library of Congress Cataloging-in-Publication Data

Yates, John, 1974–
    The incredible four-year adventure : finding real faith, fun, and friendship at college / John Yates and Chris Yates.
        p.   cm.
    Includes bibliographical references.
    ISBN 0-8010-6336-1 (pbk.)
    1. College students—Religious life. 2. Christian life. I. Yates, Chris, 1976–   . II. Title.
BV4531.2.Y38   2000
248.8'34—dc21   00-027893

Scripture quotations are from the HOLY BIBLE, NEW INTERNATIONAL VERSION®. NIV®. Copyright © 1973, 1978, 1984 by International Bible Society. Used by permission of Zondervan Publishing House. All rights reserved.

For current information about all releases from Baker Book House, visit our web site:
                    http://www.bakerbooks.com

Gratefully dedicated to Jeff Taylor,
director of student ministries at the Falls Church (Episcopal),
who, more than any other,
prepared us to take on the college experience.

CONTENTS

ACKNOWLEDGMENTS

We cannot overstate our thanks to the many individuals who journeyed alongside us in the formation of this book.

Without the generous love of our parents, John and Susan Yates, we would have no college experience to look back on. We thank them not only for footing the bill for those combined eight years (!), but for the even greater gift of modeling the Christian walk to us in all that they do.

We are particularly grateful to Steven Garber and John Stott for their pivotal advice to us in the early stages of this project and for kind encouragement along the way.

Many others have been an immense blessing and help to us as well. Thanks especially to Christy Yates, Alysia Ponzi, Allison Gaskins, Susy and Libby Yates, Collin Messer, Donald Drew, and Dean and Gail Borgman. The gift of their encouragement, advice, and prayers supplied us with the fuel to drive the vision for this project forward.

We are also indebted to Steve Griffith and Baker Books for their professional efforts in carrying this project along to publication.

Special thanks to our grandmothers, Sue Yates and Frances Alexander, for their daily prayers and for being the most faithful models of lordship, integrity, and servanthood we know.

Thanks must also go out to all of our college roommates who shared life with us and so many of the experiences and thoughts that make up this book.

ACKNOWLEDGMENTS

Finally, our greatest appreciation is reserved for those countless students and graduates who contributed the stories, reflections, and insights that make up the real content of this book. Your collective wisdom gives this project a voice and substance that is far greater than the two of us. Thank you.

INTRODUCTION

From the ABCS to the SATS it often seems the first eighteen years of our lives are spent in constant anticipation of that dream we call college. In elementary school we waited anxiously in class, watching the clock and counting the minutes until recess. When high school came around, and we'd lost the recess option, we began to look upon college as the next great playground of life. It was mysterious, new, and somehow enchanting in a grown-up kind of way.

The older you become in high school, the longer it seems to take for college to become a reality. Then suddenly, it's graduation and you step off the stage with a diploma signifying the end of the precollege era. A few short summer months fly by, you pack up the car, say good-bye to the dog, and before you know it you're meeting your roommate and suffering through freshman orientation. Voila! You are a college student.

But pause for a minute and survey the features of this playground before you. Study its faces, opportunities, risks, and challenges. Observe the games being played. Notice the people stumbling about in confusion without direction, while others walk upright, appearing focused and confident. Notice what's not there, such as family, old friends, the hometown church, and even your own feats of accomplishment. Take it all in and remind yourself that you are the same person, led by the same God. You have entered a new period in a new place, and it has the potential to be an incredible experience. As you take this pause be sure you are taking it with the Lord—

that you are willing to follow him through college as he guides and directs. Otherwise, you will fly through the college experience, and the four-year snooze button will go off with an abrupt wake-up call from the real world. What a disappointment it would be to suddenly look back on college and wonder how you wasted it, how you lost sight of what mattered, and how you found four years of wandering and worldliness.

It's true, there are as many different college experiences as there are students going to college. But regardless of what year it is or where the school is, Christian students often face a similar set of challenges and opportunities. From struggling with unfulfilled expectations to handling new sources of conflict with our faith, there is sufficient cause for arming ourselves with the resources and determination necessary for remaining fixed on God as we navigate our way through college.

Because one of the first things to happen at college is meeting what seems like ten thousand different people, we thought it fitting to introduce ourselves. We are John and Chris Yates, pleased to make your acquaintance. John is twenty-five years old and a recent graduate of the University of Virginia, where he studied religion. Chris is twenty-three and is a more recent graduate of the University of North Carolina at Chapel Hill, where he majored in history. Despite the obvious Atlantic Coast Conference rivalry, we do love each other. In fact, being at two different schools enabled us to accumulate two different college experiences, and we've enjoyed comparing notes on our observations over the past few years.

It has become increasingly clear to us that too many Christian students go off to college without adequate preparation for the challenges they will face. Perhaps you've had or heard of Christian friends going off to college and somehow losing sight of their faith. While some do experience substantial growth and strengthening of their faith in college, too many just can't seem to stay committed and get enticed by lifestyles and beliefs completely contrary to Christ. On a more practical level, there are fresh challenges in areas such as finding Christian fellowship, handling new freedoms and new responsibilities, setting priorities, and defending your faith. What we hope to provide in this book is a fresh perspective on issues such as these and some helpful tools for taking your faith with you into every area of the college experience.

Obviously we do not pretend to have all the answers or to have a seven-step program for the highly successful Christian college student. In fact, we hope that through seeing how we've struggled with certain issues and difficult questions, you will be able to more clearly understand our points. To gain as broad an understanding as possible, we've compiled advice and testimonies from students at a number of different schools—public, private, large, and small. We hope the stories we tell and the lessons that fill these pages will be helpful to you as you wrestle with the challenges so many students face. Although we have often found it necessary to change people's names to keep them anonymous, all of the stories are true, and all of the quotations are as accurate as possible.

We've divided the book into four parts, each containing several chapters. The book begins by examining the *foundation* we all need in order to pursue a godly life at college. We then turn to address the different types of *relationships* we encounter at college. Relationships are followed by the *realities* of college life and some of the practical demands that come with life on your own. Finally, we conclude the book with a section on *academics* and a look at the main reason why we're at college in the first place.

Be encouraged; we have a sure foundation to build on, and it is a great reassurance to find ourselves on the collegiate playground, jungle gyms and all, with our lives grounded in a godly foundation that transcends the obstacles set before us and the games being played around us. We hope the following pages help to strengthen that foundation in your life.

PART ONE

foundation

When we initially sat down to write this book, the first three chapters looked very different than they do now. We have always had a strong desire for this to be a practical, hands-on book, so when we first started writing, we dove in and tried to tackle the how-to questions right from the start. How do I insure I'll get along with my roommate? How do I choose the right fellowship group? How do I choose the major that's right for me? How do I resist the temptation to drink? and so on.

We were enjoying ourselves, but a problem was developing. It seemed that in trying to dish out loads of practical advice on how to be faithful at college, we were leaving out the foundation upon which a faithful life is built and from which this practical advice is gleaned.

We discussed this need for laying the foundation with different college students and graduates to see if we were on the right track. The response was unanimous: "I don't need another how-to book to tell me exactly what to do. They are always too specific in areas that don't quite relate to me. Instead, give me the tools with which to shape my *own* life at college and I will be better equipped."

Our hope in this first part of the book is to lay down that foundation and provide some of those tools. As you will see, we are still very concerned with the how-to's of living a life that is glorifying to God at college, but we realize that to discuss "How?" we first have to discuss "Why bother at all?" Throughout our conversations with students several themes began to appear and reappear. Though not everyone said things the same way or described valuable lessons they had learned with the same words, three distinct yet interrelated themes began to emerge.

These themes are *lordship, integrity*, and *servanthood*—together they form this first part, offering a foundation for the rest of the book. These three themes are central to the whole pursuit of living a godly life during the college years. We think you'll see just how practical they are as you move through them.

LORDSHIP

Two Ways to Go

CHAPTER

1

I'll never forget the atmosphere at our church youth ministry's senior dinner back in the spring before my high school graduation. Proud parents, proud ministry leaders, and even presumably a proud God all converged in the banquet hall of our church for a dinner to celebrate the graduation feats of the senior students in our youth group. Though scattered about at different high schools in the area, we seniors held a common bond through a youth group that had exploded in ever-increasing numbers and meaningful fellowship. We were faithful finishers in the eyes of our parents and leaders, and all-around superstars in our own eyes. As Jeff, the director of youth ministry, spoke from the podium about each of us, he told countless tales of our experiences together and of the spiritual growth he had seen. Jeff spoke honestly about our strengths and weaknesses, while our parents nodded in agreement and we students kidded each other about moments of great embarrassment we'd had during those four years. Central to the whole evening was a feeling that we were a strong group whose individual relationships with the Lord were grounded in the solid, unshakable foundation of faith. Bring on college!

But in the midst of it all I remember a faint feeling of insecurity trespassing on the positive atmosphere of the night: Would we all make it? Did we really know what we were getting ourselves into? Would this gallery of God-fearing students find a way through all the uncertainties of college without wandering from the footprints of our Lord?

Among those in attendance that night were two girls about to head off to large state schools in the fall. Each had demonstrated an ability to lead and motivate other students and had grown in her faith throughout the previous year. No one was worried that they wouldn't survive, and everyone expected them to thrive in their respective new atmospheres. Not more than nine months later, however, I was surprised to hear that one, Kathy, had virtually abandoned her faith, changed her lifestyle, and cut off almost all ties with Christian friends from home. Another year went by and I found out that she had dropped out of school, spent some time on a commune in the mountains, and eventually joined the ranks of those devoted to following a music group on its perpetual concert tour around the country. Meanwhile, the other girl, Elaine, was doing fine in spite of the common challenges that arise, was taking steps to grow in her faith, and was making an effort to have an effective ministry to those around her.

What happened? What was the difference between Elaine and Kathy? They both came from similar backgrounds, were leaders in their church youth group, and were respected as mature believers. What was it that enabled Elaine to maintain her faith and continue to grow throughout college while Kathy seemed to abandon everything? Although there were probably many factors involved, one key difference was their understanding of *lordship*.

One Way to Live

When asked what he wished he had been told before heading off to college for his first year, Josh captured a common theme: "There is really nothing more that I wish I had been told; I just wish I had listened better. Everyone told me that I should put Christ first in my life before I left for college, because it would be much harder once I got there to look past all the distractions and focus on him. They were right, and it took me my entire freshman year to figure that out."

In his honest response Josh hit on the most important point of lordship—*Christ comes first*. A simple principle, but one that can often take an entire year or more to finally understand. He didn't want the magic formula for a great time in college; he just wished he had listened more carefully to that fundamental advice to put Christ first. Inviting Christ to be the head of our lives is a decision for lordship. It isn't just made by college students, either; it is the defining feature in the life of anyone who calls himself or herself a Christian. "But seek *first* his kingdom and his righteousness, and all these things will be given to you as well" (Matt. 6:33).

Make no mistake, this is a basic Christian principle, but it is a ridiculous idea in the eyes of the world. Even on the most liberal of secular university campuses, where new lifestyles and belief systems are invented practically every day, it is hard to find anything more alternative or more radical than the idea of Christian lordship. Both Elaine and Kathy must have seen this to be true of their faith as they made the move from an exciting and encouraging high school ministry to the new terrain of a university campus.

During the first week at college this was a realization that hit many of our Christian friends, forcing them to ask new and difficult questions: Am I crazy to think all my decisions and actions are to be made with Christ as the head of my life? How does the faith I developed in high school fit in to the puzzle of this place? While Kathy let the insecurity caused by these questions gradually pull her away from the lordship of Christ, Elaine found relief from their sudden jolt by clinging more firmly to her Lord. Any of us could go either way. None of us can afford to assume that our faith will carry itself over the hurdles of the college playground. College forces us to a point of decision. *What we do and think in the first ten days of the first year usually points our compass in one direction or the other.*

But what, practically speaking, does it mean to call Christ lord, and what does this look like in everyday life?

We're Not So Unique After All

Karen's main ambition in college was to graduate with an engagement ring on her left hand. She succeeded, but a few short months later, when her engagement fell apart, she was left stranded without a purpose and without direction. All of her previous thought and energy had gone into getting that ring.

Martin's dream was to start a revival at his university that would sweep into every sector of the campus. What began as a Christ-centered prayer became a controlling ambition. When the movement failed to produce mass conversions, Martin was left to ponder what his motivations had become and why he suddenly felt alienated from Christians and non-Christians alike.

Calvin did everything he had to as an undergraduate to be the perfect candidate for a high-paying job. Now he spends seventy hours a week on Wall Street raking in the money but without time to spend it or friends to enjoy it with. His bank account is growing while his friendships deteriorate.

We often talk about lordship as a specifically Christian theme. But this can be misleading and often makes us feel more unique than perhaps we are. If you stop to think about it, *everyone, in their own way, has a lord of their life.* Simply defined, a lord is a master or a ruler. Karen, Martin, and Calvin all had different lords whom they served: Karen wanted a husband, Martin wanted to be a great spiritual leader, and Calvin wanted to be rich. Each of these individual ambitions became lords that mastered them. No matter how free we might think we are, there is no such thing as freedom from lordship in this life. Something will always master you. What sets us apart as Christians is that we acknowledge this truth, choose Christ as lord, and submit to him in our daily lives.

Choice, Freedom, and PB&J Sandwiches

I am always overwhelmed when I go to the grocery store. Even if I have a really detailed list, I am still confronted by the mind-numbing volume of choices available to me. Take, for example, picking out jelly for my peanut butter and jelly sandwiches. Do I want raspberry, strawberry, blackberry, or mixed fruit? Do I want jam, marmalade, or preserves? Seeds or seedless? No sugar added, or sugar added? Eight ounces or twelve? Plastic or glass? And so I stand there, frozen and confused by the number of decisions to make. And then I notice the big glass jar that has peanut butter and jelly already mixed together. Maybe I want that? Sometimes I wish there was only one kind of jelly and that the only choice involved was whether to buy it. It's enough to make a man eat tuna fish instead.

Why are there so many options? Simply put, we as a society worship the god of choice. We think that the highest good is to have an endless number of options put before us so we can personally determine what is best. This is true not only in the grocery store but in our personal and moral lives as well. We do not want to be ethically limited. Freedom of choice is our lord.

At first this doesn't sound much like lordship. We are free to do whatever we want, free from any constraints or qualifications, free from any lord. But by worshiping freedom of choice we abandon any allegiance to guidance or structure—everything becomes a spontaneous choice or consumer good. And you know what it feels like to stand frozen in the grocery store aisle with too many choices and no guidance. Wouldn't it be freeing to have the choice made for you and the only decision be to buy or not to buy? That is what submitting to the lordship of Christ is like. *In a world of mind-numbing choice, Christ says, "This is the way, walk in it," and we are left to follow or not.* There is incredible freedom in knowing what is right and simply doing it. As Jesus says in John 8:32, "You will know the truth, and the truth will set you free."

Many of us when we hear the word lordship immediately think of rules and regulations and of having to give up things in our lives we would much rather hold on to. We think that following Christ limits our freedom. This is backward. *Following Christ limits our choices but not our freedom.* In fact, real freedom is found in acknowledging truth, and in obedience—doing what is right in God's sight. We do what is right not just because he said so, though this is sufficient, but because we believe God's commands have our best interest in mind.

Of all the conceivable lords we could serve, the only one that has our best interest in mind is Christ. We may not always agree with what he determines is best, but we abide in him regardless. Having been made by him and redeemed by him, we belong to him and trust in his will. All other masters manipulate us in one way or another, ultimately leading to disappointment and despair. True freedom is found only in the lordship of Christ. For in Christ we are free to become the person he has created us to be.

Back Dives and Trust Falls

As a kid I spent many a summer afternoon at the neighborhood pool, soaking up the good life of warm weather and cold Italian ices from the snack bar. I was frequently drawn to the opportunities and challenges posed by the diving boards. It was the challenge of doing a back dive that beckoned me most. Some of you who are more acrobatically inclined may see the back dive as hardly a challenge, but it's a big deal for a nine-year-old. Trembling there on the edge of the board, the most eerie feeling of all was caused by the fact that I was facing backward. It's one thing to run and fling yourself headfirst into the spacious depths of the deep end, but another thing entirely to face the trees and fall backward into the water. I had been told by our local poolside experts to simply arch my back, raise my arms, and look for the water. Sounded easy enough. Whatever!

After many messy attempts, I managed to get used to the awkwardness of it all and finally landed the dive. The hardest part for me was simply committing to the point where my hands were over my head, my knees bent, and my back arched beyond the point of no return. It was that feeling of helplessness between the firm security of the board and the relief of feeling my hands slice through the water that I found so hard to face. Before I could perfect my technique I had to learn how to commit to the dive, let go, keep my eyes focused on the water, and surrender to the force of gravity.

Committing to the lordship of Christ is a lot like learning to do a back dive. We are accustomed to facing one direction in life in which we are in control and the benefits of what lies ahead seem pretty obvious. The diving board is like a runway from which we eagerly launch ourselves into anything and everything we want. We do it again and again. We can enter the water differently every time, but we are always facing the same direction. To walk to the very edge of the board and turn to face the other way—focusing our entire attention on that which had previously been behind us—is a radical step. Even though the gap between the end of the board and the surface of the water is only a few feet, it feels like a free fall into the unknown.

Lordship involves surrender. It is like falling backward, but with a purpose—into the arms of a God who you know is there and will catch you. This is a far cry from those trust-fall exercises everyone does at some point in school. You know the ones, where you are forced to place your life in the hands of a small group of potentially inept peers.

Trust falls aside, there is fear in falling, as in surrendering, because it is an unnatural and uncomfortable event. But God's grace has made it possible for us to abandon the self-centered direction of our lives, do an about-face, and fall under the direction and control of his lordship. Those who look with bitterness at all of the giving up they might have to do if they become a Christian are stuck in the routine of running down the diving board in the same direction, unaware of the excitement and joy that come with a changed perspective.

Long Days, Longer Nights

I was once told that if you can go to bed at night after a busy day and still have a peaceful state of mind, you are probably getting along pretty well in life. Sadly, that was almost never the case for me during my freshman year at the University of North Carolina. When the distractions of the day on campus had ceased and I headed to bed, I was left wrestling with two basic questions. The first was: How am I going to do everything that I'm supposed to do tomorrow?

My attempts to mentally go down the to-do list for the next day left me frustrated with myself for taking on too much and angry at myself for not being capable of actually doing it all. The advice a friend recently gave to incoming freshmen would have served me well: "Instead of getting involved in tons of activities, pick a couple of things to which you can really devote yourself and where you can make a real difference for the Lord." *My problem was that I had come to believe that the more I did, the better I was.*

The second question I grappled with blazed across a page of my journal that fall: Who am I!? Perhaps it was provoked by my inability to answer the first question and my resulting insecurity. Or perhaps it was because for the first time in my life no one knew who I had been in high school and no one seemed to care. The guy I thought I was no longer seemed so convincing, and the new image I had of myself was confused. There had to be some achievement, some personality trait, some academic ability or social feat I could stake myself to as an anchor for my identity.

Needless to say, all this midnight worrying prevented me from getting the sleep I needed. "Are you getting enough rest and taking good care of yourself?" my mom would often ask over the phone in a concerned motherly way. "Of course, I'm fine," I habitually responded. When I came home for Christmas break and was diagnosed with mononucleosis ("mono" for short), it was clear I'd been bluffing.

Each of us is familiar with these two questions in one version or another. They are especially common among college students and conveniently provide a clear window into two great issues of lordship: identity and purpose. Let's look first at the question of "Who am I?" and then work backward to "How am I going to accomplish everything set before me?"

Identity

College is a breeding ground for identity crises. Every student has in one way or another been uprooted from where they were, and who they were, and dropped off at the campus playground, left to figure out who they are now going to be. There is a giddy sense of opportunity at college because, essentially, you can be whatever and whoever you want. You can create and re-create yourself again and again.

As Christians we have already been re-created in Christ, and we regard ourselves as the workmanship of God. "Therefore, if anyone is in Christ, he is a new creation," Paul excitedly wrote to the church in Corinth. "The old has gone, the new has come!" (2 Cor. 5:17). Our identity is never up to us alone; it is forever joined with

Christ, and we are new creations specifically designed and restored by God. *This does not mean we are immune from having a crisis of identity; it simply means we don't need to re-create ourselves.* Christ has already done this. College is a time of discovering who we already are in Christ rather than manufacturing custom images.

For all my efforts at answering the question "Who am I?" during my freshman year, the only thing that brought progress was asking another question: "Who is Christ?" I finally made the realization that who I am has everything to do with who Christ is, and who God has made me through him. The same God to whom I have surrendered, in whom I have put my total trust, is the lord of my identity. As Paul says in his letter to the Galatians, "I have been crucified with Christ and I no longer live, but Christ lives in me" (Gal. 2:20).

Jesus wanted to make sure his disciples knew this basic concept when he was speaking to them one afternoon (Luke 9:18–27). "Who do you say I am?" Jesus asked. Peter responded with an answer that, though brief, would have been enough to have all of them executed for blasphemy by the Jewish community or for sedition by the Romans. He called him "the Christ of God." In effect he was saying, "Well, Jesus, we believe that you are the one who was promised long ago by our prophets and teachers; you are the final great king of the Jewish people, and the Son of God come down as a man."

As an affirmation of what Peter had said, Jesus took the title "Son of Man" for himself and proceeded to explain how he "must suffer many things and be rejected by the elders, chief priests and teachers of the law, and he must be killed and on the third day be raised to life." He went on to caution them, saying, "If anyone would come after me, he must deny himself and take up his cross daily and follow me. For whoever wants to save his life will lose it, but whoever loses his life for me will save it. *What good is it for a man to gain the whole world, and yet lose or forfeit his very self?*"

What Jesus said was difficult because it involved commitment and sacrifice, but there was even more to it. Jesus was making a phenomenal promise here. He was saying, "If you believe that I am indeed God's Son, and if you commit yourself to following me, you will gain more than you could ever imagine. In giving your life to me you will gain *true* life, identity, and purpose. Because who you are, 'your very self,' is completely wrapped up in who you say I am."

My brother, John, keeps a very short poem that he wrote during his first year of college taped to the bookshelf in his room. It is strategically placed so that he sees it every time he walks into the room.

> "Who am I?" I cried.
> And silence answered back.
> "Who are you?" I gasped.
> And peace came breathing in.
> In "I Am," "Who am I?" finds its answer.

("I Am" is a phrase God uses to describe himself in the Old Testament: "I AM WHO I AM" [Exod. 3:14].)

Purpose

In the fall of my sophomore year I took an introductory course in psychology. The main thing the course taught me was that I didn't want to be a psychology major! One of the interesting things I did manage to learn was the view held by some psychologists that there are three basic emotional needs every human being shares: (1) the need to be known, (2) the need to be loved, and (3) the need to have a purpose in life. Whether or not people admit it, these needs are amplified during our college years, and the rush to re-create ourselves is the usual attempt to meet these needs.

If we are Christians, it is easy to see how Jesus meets the first two needs. He is God and thereby knows us because he made us, and he showed his love for us by dying on the cross. Simple. But how does he give us purpose? Christ gives us purpose, because in acknowledging that Jesus is God and pledging to follow him, we identify ourselves with him, and *he becomes our purpose in life.* His greater glory becomes our supreme concern.

So how does this help me to sort out the far more practical question of "How am I going to accomplish everything set before me?" The reason we've spent so much time on identity is because purpose is bound up in identity.

When we asked our friend Josh if there was anything he regretted doing or not doing in college, he said he had tried to do *everything,* and "at times I have spread myself too thin and have not been able to be as effective as I would have liked to be, or as effective as the Lord would have liked me to be." In our culture, busyness is thought to convey significance—if I am a busy person I must be an important person. However true it may be that important and influential people tend to be busy, God does not command us to be busy. *God doesn't need us to be overcommitted in order to please him.*

Often when we are always busy, our focus is on what we do, and not on who we are. The Christian calling, however, is primarily one of *being* rather than doing. Christ calls us to "be holy, because I am holy" (1 Peter 1:16). He didn't say, "Be busy doing good, because I am busy doing good." Our focus needs to be directed much more toward who we are rather than what we do. Instead of worrying all the time about "What am I going to do tomorrow?" we should instead ask the question "Who would Christ have me *be* right now?"

Of course, you can't escape having to make those difficult decisions of what extracurricular activities to get involved in, which clubs to join, and how many classes to take (these are issues we will spend time on later in the book), but you can face such questions with a much higher level of peace when you see that ultimately the significance of what you do is secondary to the primary issue of who you are. "But seek *first* his kingdom and his righteousness, and all these things will be given to you as well" (Matt. 6:33).

Questions for Study and Reflection

Study passages: Philippians 3:7–11

1. What are the things or people in your life that most influence or define who you are?

2. In general terms, what does *lordship* mean to you? How does it differ from what is meant by the term *savior?*

3. What are some lords you see in the people around you? In yourself?

4. How is the lordship of Christ unique? How does it impact the way you live each day?

INTEGRITY

Stephen's Story

Stephen arrived at the University of Virginia confident he would make a big splash, meet lots of great people, join a good fraternity, and have fun while earning a top-notch degree. Like many of us, Stephen came from a Christian background. Having been involved in a strong youth group, he knew his Bible pretty well and was seen as a solid Christian. He was an attractive, bright, and likable guy. Yet during his first semester, he fell flat on his face.

Fraternity rush at UVA starts right away first year. You herd off to Rugby Road, where the fraternity houses are, most nights of the week with all of the other first-year guys, hoping to make a good impression and get accepted. Stephen made it through rush and accepted a bid at one of the most popular fraternities. It was on bid night, when he accepted the invitation to join the fraternity and begin the long process of pledging, that Stephen made his first big mistake. We'll let him take over the story.

"At my fraternity, pledges are asked to chug a pint of Jim Beam whiskey on bid night. Before the festivities were to begin, hordes of brothers made a point of grabbing me and telling me that I did not have to participate. Some even offered to drink for me. Not good enough for me. At that point something clicked within. I did not want to just be one of the fellas at the house. I felt like a good Christian could not be 'the man,' but I would settle for being nothing less. Hence, the beginning of the end. I drank all of my pint and got lit up like a Christmas tree. *I made a conscious choice to step away from the Lord.*"

After that first night, Stephen had a reputation at the fraternity he was keen on maintaining. But he also had Christian friends and a small group to impress. "In an effort to be 'the man,' I still tried to play it from all ends," says Stephen. "I continued in my small group and figured I could fool everyone. Act like a Christian among Christians and be a pagan when among pagans. I referred to it as my 'when in Rome' attitude. . . . I made my own decisions, and I knew exactly what I was doing. I did not believe that a Christian could survive and be respected in the world, especially the intense college social scene. . . . My goals were warped, and I paid the consequences. . . . I knew my choice [to drink] was not the best from God's perspective, but I wanted to be 'the man.' Ironically, the brothers respected me for my faith and eventually despised me for my drunkenness."

Three weeks later, Stephen was kicked out of the fraternity, in large part because of his drinking. At the same time, he had to face his small group and tell them he'd been living a double life. All at once it seemed his world was crashing down around him. And all he had been doing was trying to fit in.

David's Challenge

When graduation season rolls around, one is likely to hear quite a collection of commencement speeches: The future rests on your shoulders—keep them strong! Let your dreams take you to new heights! Life's a party and we've just finished setting up! Rarely do the messages actually stick with us. But at a recent high school graduation, David gave a speech to his fellow classmates that we hope they will not soon forget. "We must be willing to make sacrifices for our beliefs," he challenged them. "We must find simple, irrefutable truths and never compromise them. . . . Even the most intricate and well-thought-out belief system is worthless if it does not change the way we act." Without even saying the word, David made a convincing call for *integrity* in the lives of his classmates.

Integrity is one of those words politicians use when they want to make a good impression. Perhaps that is why most of us cringe when we hear it. There are many ways in which our modern culture misunderstands and misuses the notion of integrity. As a result it has lost a lot of its meaning and significance. People are tired of hearing about something they can't see and don't understand. For those who desire to live a life glorifying to God, however, integrity is crucial.

Most people, if they stop to think about it, understand integrity to include such virtues as honesty, trustworthiness, and responsibility. These are all core qualities for a Christian to possess, and they are a part of integrity, but this isn't all that integrity involves.

Integrity Involves Integration

Both of us are color-blind, but this doesn't mean that we only see black and white. We are simply stuck at a preschool level of color recognition and are often confused. Growing up we were very thankful that Crayola labeled their crayons. As a result of our color-blindness, we have a hard time matching clothes. Neither of us ever goes shopping alone. Chris once wore what he thought were a pair of black loafers to church, only to have pointed out to him that one was brown. The challenge for us each morning is to make sure our clothes match, that they blend together nicely—that they are integrated with one another.

Personal integrity is like having a good sense of fashion. It is a deliberate interrelating of every facet of life so that who we are, what we think, and how we act match and make sense together. Integration happens when our beliefs are evident in our behavior and when our behavior is consistent with our beliefs. In other words, what we say and what we do should be sending the same message. *Because the lordship of Christ covers all areas of our lives, he must be lord of both our beliefs and our behavior.*

Stephen's story is like that of many students who arrive at college lacking two crucial tools: (1) a firm and deep commitment to stated beliefs, and (2) an awareness of the need for making those beliefs consistent with behavior. "It is important to take a harsh look at yourself now," our friend Scott recently said to a group of high school seniors. "Know where your security is and see that it is in the Lord. Before you *go* to college decide which *way* you will go when you get there. Be willing to take a stand and *act* on what you believe. Remember that little compromises lead to big ones—form the right habits now." After one year in college surrounded by friends like Stephen, Scott knew this need all too well.

Does integrating our beliefs and our behavior mean we should avoid at all costs going into any tempting or worldly environment? No, it means that *our beliefs must guide our behavior regardless of where we go and whom we are with.* As integrated people, actually we have great freedom of movement, because who we are is not dictated by where we go, our peers, or our circumstances. We can feel free to join fraternities, sororities, and other non-Christian organizations without hesitation only *if* we understand this principle.

As people of integrity living "in the world, but not of the world," we must integrate our relationships and activities. Stephen immersed himself in an environment that ate away at his faith. He showed a lack of integrity (not to mention wisdom) by thinking he could get away with ignoring God in one part of his life. This is one side of the coin. On the other side, too many Christian students go to the opposite extreme, entirely separating and isolating themselves from the "secular" world of college life. Granted, none of us needs to be rushing toward temptation, but at the same time we shouldn't be running away from non-Christian situations with an "us against them" mentality.

Early in my freshman year some of the guys on my hall made me promise that I would go to at least two fraternity parties with them before our fall break (apparently I had been isolating myself a little too much). I agreed. On both outings two things struck me: (1) The simple fact that I was actually joining them for the evening instead of clinging to my Christian friends or hiding out in my room meant something to them, and (2) while immersed in the scene at the parties I felt the Lord affirming the fact that I belonged to him—that even though I was in the world, I was still a stranger to it. Thus, *to live as people of integrity, we need to draw boundaries, but we don't need to build barriers.*

The Opposite of Integration Is Compromise and Compartmentalization

Stephen's strategy was to keep God in one part of his life and not let him into the others. Although his first big mistake was getting drunk on bid night, his problems began long before. He came to school with a "take it as it comes" attitude about ethical decisions. Before getting drunk he had begun drinking small amounts at parties. This initial compromise only made him vulnerable to more, and before long he was not the same person who had shown up at college a few months earlier. *Stephen was setting himself up for a fall by neglecting to set boundaries.*

Without a conscious effort on our part to set and keep boundaries, we will naturally take part in the sin of the world around us. Paul challenges the Christians in Rome when he senses they are falling into this trap. He says to them, "Do not conform any longer to the pattern of this world, but be transformed by the renewing of your mind. Then you will be able to test and approve what God's will is—his good, pleasing and perfect will" (Rom. 12:2). Here again we see the value of Scott's advice. If we don't decide on certain things before we go, when faced by a decision in the heat of the moment, our sinful human nature will almost always take over and we will compromise. Drinking is just one example. Sex is the same way. There are few places in the world where sex is easier to come by. In co-ed dorms with girls and guys in and out of bedrooms at all hours, who would notice anyway? Let's be honest, the hormonal potential at college is tremendous. If we haven't made a vow not to have premarital sex before going off to school, then the chances of giving in to temptation are that much higher as we adapt to the standards of people around us. Even at a Christian college temptation remains alive and well.

One of the keys to avoiding dangerous compromise is refusing to have different standards for different compartments of our lives. We must let God into everything. Academic activities, social activities, on-campus events, and fellowship activities should all be permeated by the same living faith. Christ is the same lord of our lives when we are in a group or by ourselves, when we are in church or in the classroom. Thank goodness we do not have to keep adjusting our standards depending on where we are and what we're doing! Keep in mind, though, compartmentalization is often subtle—we quietly allow ourselves to keep the lordship standards of one area from affecting us in another area. Just because we're not getting drunk or having sex doesn't mean we are necessarily doing okay. We can avoid these "big" sins and still keep God in a box in a little corner compartment of our lives, switching him on and off as we move from activity to activity or person to person. Sounds pretty grim doesn't it?

For the most part, freshmen who come through their first year without falling prey to the temptations of compartmentalization are those who have decided *before* ever setting foot on campus what they will and will not allow themselves to do. Having just finished her second year in college, Jane encourages us along these lines: "The only advice I was given before coming to college," Jane said with a half-grin on her face, "was an admonition that college was full of 'alcoholics' and 'sex mongers.' If students know what they believe and know the tools for evaluating the circumstances in which they are placed . . . college life is much easier. Really, it is not that hard if you keep your focus in the right place. *Keeping your focus is the challenge; college is just the location.*" A life of integrity is an integrated life in which there are no boundaries to the lordship of Christ.

Structural Integrity

Another way of thinking about integrity is to look at it from the perspective of an engineer. When you are building a bridge, road, house, or high-rise, you have to insure that each part is working in conjunction with every other part. If one section of a bridge has a bad patch of concrete, the whole bridge is weakened. If one steel girder in the roof of an apartment building is incorrectly placed, the whole building is in danger of coming to pieces. All engineers and architects know that unless every detail of the building is attended to, the whole structure will be worthless. This is called structural integrity.

As Christians we look to God as the chief engineer of our lives. In creating us he has given our bodies structural, or physical, integrity. But this is not all he desires. God also wants all the various components of our day-to-day lives—friendships, academic work, home life, and so on—to fit together into a secure and integrated whole. This often means taking a deliberate step to look at the details of our daily life and insure that they are not at odds with one another, seeing that each part of our life has been tested and examined so it fits fully under the lordship of Christ.

Our friend Lane is a very driven and committed student. It frustrated her, however, to find that life in the classroom seemed so distant and unrelated to her faith. How could she make it fit with the whole of her life? Academics is a passion for Lane, and finding no real guidance for how to combine that passion with her passion for the Lord, it was up to her to be creative and deliberate. "The best thing I did," she now reflects, "was try to sit down after every class I attended and every book I studied and consider how the academic experience related to my life and faith. I made an effort to integrate things by reflecting on them in a kind of academic journal." She was not content to let one corner of her life stand apart from the rest, and instead took deliberate steps toward wholeness. Just as the structure of a building requires integrity, or wholeness, the call to live a godly and holy life necessitates the integration of every detail of our lives under the lordship of Christ.

There is no way to anticipate all of the new and different challenges students will encounter at college. But we can prepare for them before ever getting there. If we have already taken a stand on certain issues, we will find it much easier to take a stand in other areas. The fact that we name Christ as our lord sets us apart and sends us on a path that requires integrity. *We cannot be Christian chameleons at college or anywhere else in our lives. We must not let the way other people live and act and make decisions determine how we are going to live.* It would be all too easy to live for the lowest common denominator—the beliefs that require the least from us. But it is more exciting, more daring, and far more meaningful to live by the standards set by the lord of our lives.

As David concluded in his graduation speech, "It is difficult enough to die for what we believe, but to truly live . . . to walk every step in accordance with our words, and to speak every word to the purpose of helping others to gain an understanding, perhaps that is harder still." Indeed, that is integrity.

So What Happened to Stephen?

Getting kicked out of the fraternity was a pretty loud wake-up call for Stephen. He knew something was wrong and that his life needed fixing. Over the next few months he was challenged in his small group to change a lot of things about his life. It wasn't easy, but over time things turned around. Through faithful friends, and a newfound understanding of the need for integrity, things began to change.

At the end of his first year Stephen had grown so much he was asked to become a volunteer leader with Young Life, working with students at a local high school. Over the next three years he poured himself into the lives of those students. Stephen later said, "My rough first year was my major motivation for leading. I did not want to see another high-schooler inflict the same pain upon himself that I inflicted upon myself. . . . Being in ministry was good for me. I realized that I was an ambassador for Christ and I had to act as such. It kept me accountable. . . . I knew that I could not fool God on this one."

When asked what he would say to a group of students about to head off to college, Stephen responded, "Integrity has to be something that one is committed to before one steps on a college campus. My focuses were elsewhere (for example: building a lot of friends and being well liked), and as a result I caved in quickly. There is no way anyone can survive if God, and living for him, is not number one. If not, compromises will come quickly. Don't fool yourself. Let my testimony speak for that. Remember, the greatest irony in this whole deal was that the brothers at my fraternity accepted me for who I was in Christ. They hated me for trying to follow them. God is attractive to others. Young Christians need to believe that and be reaffirmed in that."

Questions for Study and Reflection

Study passages: Daniel 1; Matthew 5:13–16

1. In your own words, describe integrity. Is it primarily a belief, an action, or both?

2. What decisions or beliefs set you apart from those around you? Does your behavior match your beliefs in those areas?

3. What issues in your life that demand integrity need to be addressed before you begin college? Drinking? Sex? Fellowship? What do you think will be the most difficult challenge?

4. What steps can you take now to decrease the temptations you are likely to face? Once you have made a decision for integrity, who will support you and hold you accountable?

SERVANTHOOD

Expectations and Disappointments

The summer before Charlotte went off to college, she was glowing with excitement and anticipation. Though slightly nervous, she had great visions of the new life that awaited her at Vanderbilt University.

I remember talking to her that summer and seeing familiar glimpses of how I felt the summer before journeying to UNC. It was that look of, "I've put up with high school long enough; bring on the new world! It's bound to be incredible." After all, college is the reward for waiting and drudging through four years of high school. It is the culmination of all previous academic efforts, and the first real experience of "freedom" from our parents.

The following spring, Charlotte reflected on her first year. "This has been an intense year for me. God has shown and taken me through heights and depths I've never seen." It is hard to expect intensity. It is hard to plan or prepare for it. Charlotte, like so many of us, expected the heights but had to adjust to the depths. Other students agreed that many of the surprises awaiting them at college were negative as well as positive.

When Brian went off to a small Christian college in Southern California, his expectations were quickly dismantled. "I was shocked to find at a Christian college the same characteristics I was trying to avoid by not going to a secular college. One friend of mine was addicted to cocaine. Girls were getting date-raped.

It was a myth that the school was a perfect place." Although his college was thought to be a safe haven of sorts from the harassing temptations and cruelty of the world, Brian discovered it had its own dark realities.

When Shervin graduated and headed off to college, there were forty other students from his high school class joining him as freshmen at the same university. Obviously, he thought, friendships he had with many of them would easily remain intact. That wasn't the case, and by the end of his first semester he found he was out of touch with nearly all of them. "It alarmed me," he said. "Those friendships were supposed to keep moving along beautifully, but they just seemed to vanish."

In each of these anecdotes there is evidence of an essential principle: *You will be disappointed by something or someone at college.* No matter how we look at it, the college experience has a lot to live up to, and some of the biggest struggles people have during the first year of school are a direct result of unrealistic expectations. We often set high expectations without even realizing it, and it doesn't take long to see that the college we've built up in our minds is hardly the college we encounter. Some of us are more susceptible to these disappointments than others, but most of us fall for them one way or another.

One friend of mine fell especially hard. She thought college was going to be a blissful paradise. She couldn't imagine anything better than life on her own, financed by Mom, with the freedom to do whatever she wanted. After August finally came and she was off to school, it was a while before I heard how she was doing. Then word got back to me that she was absolutely miserable. She had banked everything on college being the answer to all of life's shortcomings. But when she realized she wasn't best friends with everyone on her hall, when she failed a test because she had skipped class half a dozen times, and when contrary to all previous thoughts she actually felt homesick, she knew she was going to hate it.

It is easy to call her expectations foolish, but those of you already in college may detect a familiar thread in our friend's story. One of the things we all look forward to is freedom. Even if you love your family, you are still anticipating the freedom that comes from being on your own. As a part of this anticipation you can't wait to be away from home, where no one cares how many taped episodes of *The Simpsons* you watch, where no one cares if you play computer games or do a little napping instead of going to class, where no one cares whether you come in before 1:00 A.M. Ahhh . . . bliss!

But wait. What about the other side of this coin? *No one cares . . .* That's right. It is nice only being responsible for yourself, but at the same time you don't have any of the security that comes from having people around you who know you well and care for you, be they friends or family. At college *no one cares* if you are eating alone in the dining hall, *no one cares* if you are lost and ten minutes late for class, *no one cares* if you are having trouble making friends. With expectations come disappointments; in freedom there is often unfamiliar loneliness.

Moving Away from "Me"

All of this talk about shattered expectations and miserable freedom is not quite as harsh as it may sound. In addition to the need for forming realistic expectations, there is a more important lesson to be learned from all of this. The root of the problem of dashed expectations is that almost everyone sees college as a time for *me.* Even our most general expectations are framed with ourselves in the foreground of the picture. It is easily the most naturally selfish time in a person's life. We have no one to look after except ourselves; we are there to increase our personal knowledge; we are living in a world that caters to our every desire; everyone is roughly our age and often interested in the same things we are; and if we happen to screw up, we may be the only ones seriously affected. The way college is set up, we don't have to care about other people, nor are we ever really encouraged to. This is the root of the problem.

We have already discussed how the currents of college life tend to pull students into habits of re-creating themselves. Compromises are made, compartments are built, and a typical student begins to wonder who he is or who he has become. The process of moving from freshman orientation to this gradual disorientation is helped along by the attractiveness of selfish living. Even if we are not terribly self-centered people, this predicament is hard to avoid. Campus orientation programs give, more or less, the same message: "Welcome to our university; here is what you can do for yourself during the next four years." The seeds of selfishness within us are heavily watered, and we innocently assume that's just how college is. We are the center of our own attention. Soon it becomes all too easy to implicitly consider friendships, dating relationships, campus activities, social activities, and academic priorities as doorways to our own gain and indulgence.

Lordship and integrity both say no to this attitude and the lifestyle it permits. We belong to God and are called to a higher standard than collegiate selfishness can afford. Not only do we see ourselves as servants of God, we also see in Christ the complete opposite of the "me first" mentality and the elevation of serving others instead.

What we have found is that the people who are most content at college, those who are happiest to be there and as a result are the most fun to be around, are those who realize they are there for a reason bigger than their own gain. Where *lordship* looks at our relationship with God and *integrity* looks at the relationship between our beliefs and behavior, *servanthood* sees lordship and integrity as the criterion for how we interact with the world around us. *It is those people who are committed to following Christ, and as a result are committed to the ideal of service, who make the most of college for themselves and for those around them.*

We know, it sounds like a real Sunday school answer, but it is the truth. We go to college expecting joy and fulfillment to come not from the college life but through Christ. Because of this we walk down a path of servanthood that leads us in the steps of the Lord and leaves a very real mark on the lives of those around us. Servants have few expectations regarding their own happiness. They are there for others, to help, to share, and to sacrifice. There's no need to get carried away and mass produce "Loving All, Serving All" T-shirts, or "Here for Jesus" buttons. Instead, we must consciously and quietly make ourselves available to the people around us and the opportunities the Lord might give us to serve them.

Living It Out

So, practically speaking, what does this mean and how is it done? Here are some thoughts: On Friday afternoon do you begin to panic at the fact that you don't have any plans of your own for the night, or are you more concerned about Dwayne down the hall, who hardly ever gets out? When you walk into the dining hall do you immediately start scanning the tables for a familiar face, or do you consider eating with that person at the corner table who always eats alone? Do you go over and offer to take home the guy you barely know from your dorm who is puking in the bushes after a "great" night out? Do you even consider offering to go to a class you're not in to take notes for a sick friend? These are just some thoughts. Looking at servanthood on a practical level provides a good wake-up call, alerting us to consider the bottom-line question: What am I here for?

One of the best arguments and examples we can give for servanthood is reporting on how the servanthood of others has impacted our lives. Think of the ways in which your life has been affected by people who are devoted to you, who are interested in you, who want to know how you are really doing, who want to help meet your practical needs. Isn't it wonderful to know such people? They model the heart of God by their desire to wash the feet of those around them. When Christ knelt down to wash the feet of the disciples, he demonstrated his commitment to servanthood by meeting a very real need. Those guys had some pretty dirty feet, mind you, but Jesus saw in them an invitation to serve.

For three years Damon had the challenging task of being my roommate. We were both a little too busy for our own good and as a result found that we hardly ever had enough quality time together. This, however, didn't stop him from being a truly faithful friend. While I was preoccupied with work at the student newspaper, in student government, or locked away in the library trying to catch up on history assignments, Damon was having to balance the needs of his academic course load with his incredible desire to encourage and serve other students. He would devote an immense amount of time each week to students at the local high school where he was a Young Life leader and frequently pray for them as well. He would go out of his way to include guys on our hall in various activities and meals together. Damon built bridges with friendships because he had the heart of a servant. He was always conscious of when people's birthdays were, and I will never forget returning home one evening to find he had pulled about fifty friends together (even out-of-town friends) for a huge celebration in my honor.

I am not the type to telephone someone just to find out how they are doing, or to make lunch plans "just to catch up on things." Heidi, however, does this with the energy of a marathon runner and the sincerity of a true friend. Even her e-mails from across campus are full of encouragement. I can say with pride that she was one of my best friends at UNC, and at the same time I know scores of other people who would say the same thing. How? It's simple, really; she remembered everyone's name and was genuinely interested in how everyone was doing. One afternoon I sat and visited with Heidi on a central part of campus, and in one hour I must have met at least twelve new friends. Nearly everyone who walked by was greeted with a jubilant hello from Heidi—and she knew *all* their names. Her outgoing and compassionate spirit kept her so busy talking with people that getting to class on time became a real challenge for her.

Ruthie has many abilities, but she is great at two things in particular: encouraging people and baking cookies. During the fall semester of her sophomore year she found an ideal way to combine both abilities and reach her campus in the process. Living in one of the many high-rise dorms that are home to one thousand students, Ruthie sensed the need to help promote some feeling of community among her many neighbors. So every Tuesday afternoon she made the kitchen on her hall a workshop for baking as many cookies as possible and that same evening hosted Cookie Tuesday in the lounge on her floor. All students were welcome to join the feast—free of charge. Eventually word spread and students from across campus were making the weekly journey.

Seeing It Through

Servanthood can take many forms. On a college campus its most obvious outlets come in the form of meeting other people's basic needs. Damon demonstrated a genuine desire to be involved in other people's lives in an inclusive, prayerful, and encouraging way. Heidi served others by giving them a meaningful sense of being known and appreciated. Ruthie made use of her skills to offer a true gift to anyone hungry for a little dessert and some conversation with other students.

We're not advocating a legalistic approach to servanthood in which we sit down at the end of the day and judge ourselves according to a special checklist. However, attaining the general attitude and discipline of servanthood is very much a day-to-day, person-by-person goal. Many people see the value of servanthood in a purely utilitarian way, "If you scratch my back, I'll scratch yours," and expect to be compensated in the end for all of their good deeds. A second trap still others fall into is that their "service" is really just another form of self-righteousness whereby they pat themselves on the back for their own good deeds. In his book *Issues Facing Christians Today* John Stott warns against the danger of seeing servanthood as a means to such selfish ends and reminds readers of the truth in T. W. Manson's statement: "In the Kingdom of God service is not a stepping-stone to nobility: it *is* nobility, the only kind of nobility that is recognized."

As it was for Christ, and is for us as Christians, genuine servanthood is a tall order. If we are going to model Christ and his love at college, this is the way to start. Moving past the infatuation with "me" is the first crucial step in denying ourselves and taking up our cross daily as we follow Christ's lead into the college world (Luke 9:23). This lifestyle is obviously not always an easy thing, and it may be frustrating, challenging, and an altogether unappreciated way to live at times. But it is the right attitude to have and the way we are meant to approach the world. It is the avenue by which we can be enthusiastically content in serving the Lord and letting him change the world around us. The best question to ask ourselves to determine our true motives behind serving is, Who is my audience while I am doing this? Who am I performing for? If the answer is anyone other or more than God, something is wrong.

Still wondering whatever happened to the girl who thought college would be heaven and came home after the first semester thinking it was more like hell? You will be happy to know she actually started to like it second semester. When she left home to return to school after Christmas break, she cried because she didn't want to go back. But when she left for home at the end of second semester, she cried because she didn't want to leave. That may seem like an incredible turnaround, but it is actually not too uncommon. School can be tough; that first semester can be difficult and surprisingly lonely, and adjusting often takes longer than we think. With these realistic expectations in mind, go with the attitude of a servant and you will be marked by a sense of peace and contentment.

Questions for Study and Reflection

Study passages: Philippians 2:1–8; Acts 20:24

1. List as many traits of a servant as you can. In what ways was Jesus a servant?

2. Who in your life has demonstrated the heart of a servant? How have they done this?

3. Why is humility so important in servanthood? What does it mean to "consider others better than yourselves"?

4. What impact will developing a spirit of service have for you in your own life each day? How will it affect your character and lifestyle in the long run?

5. What are some practical ways you can serve others this week? What people would least expect to be served by you?

PART TWO

relationships

At a 1997 conference in Marburg, Germany, sponsored by the International Fellowship of Evangelical Students, over twenty-five hundred students from forty-one European nations gathered to talk about faith and life at college. As an adopted citizen of the United Kingdom, I attended and was invigorated by my time there. Christian students came from countries as different as Azerbaijan and Austria, and I was struck by the diversity of the body of Christ. And yet while being impressed by the diversity of the group, I was even more surprised to discover just how similar college students are all over the world.

During the week, two hundred of the students participated in a workshop on how to care for their fellow students. As a part of this workshop, the students filled out a survey that asked them to list the top concerns and struggles faced by students in their home country. The struggle that topped the list for students all over Europe was *the painful problem of loneliness.* In fact, roughly half of all the problems cited were relational in nature. College is supposed to be a wonderful time of building deep and lasting relationships, but it is obviously much harder than many of us anticipate. The struggle with loneliness clearly is found all over the world.

This problem of loneliness is symptomatic of the great emphasis we put on relationships at college. So much of our first year at school is taken up simply with meeting new people and trying to remember their names. Roommates, hallmates, classmates, fellow dorm residents, fellow club members, friends, friends of friends, professors, and graduate assistants—just to name a few of the new relationships to be developed. And this is not to mention friends from high school, boyfriends, girlfriends, and the family at home. It's exhausting just thinking about it.

Since relationships of all different kinds are central to the college experience, we've devoted a whole section of the book to this topic. Starting with the central relationships in our lives, we work outward in an ever-widening circle trying to bring them all into focus, constantly assessing how they might come under the lordship of Christ, be fully integrated parts of who we are, and be means by which we might model the servant nature of Christ.

ME, MYSELF, AND GOD

Phone Bills and E-mail

A good relationship with your sister can sometimes be costly. Susy and Libby, our twin sisters, are best friends. So when going off to college meant going off to two different places, our family wondered how they would handle the separation. It was to be the first time they had been apart for more than two weeks since they were born. Would they survive on their own? Would one transfer?

When just one month of college had passed, they both complained about the diminishing size of their bank accounts. After we pressed her for more information, Susy told us the amount of her phone bill, and we immediately understood. Libby confessed to having similar fees. They had been calling each other almost every day! After years of unhindered daily communication, they weren't about to let the new reality of geographic separation prevent them from filling each other in on every aspect of daily life. Even at the end of their first year they were still talking every day, though it was through the slightly more cost effective means of e-mail rather than by phone. Without realizing it our sisters were demonstrating the very simple principle that *in meaningful relationships, regular communication is essential.*

The same principle applies to our relationship with God. "College is a great place to deepen relationships and develop new ones. But as a Christian your most important relationship is your relationship with God . . . daily quiet times and prayer are essential," says Jim. Another student agrees and warns that "your faith will come crashing down around you unless you commit to spending quality time with God on your own."

Our contact with God isn't by phone or by e-mail sent to god@heaven.com. It is more direct and personal, ideally becoming a kind of constant interaction. If we are seeking to be people who live under the lordship of Christ, who integrate faith into every aspect of life, and who aspire to live a life of service, we will have a deep need for spiritual motivation and energy. This only comes within the context of consistent, open communication with our creator and redeemer who, when we meet him face-to-face, gives us the motivation and the energy to live godly lives.

Survival Skills and Early Mornings

At the beginning of my last year at the University of Virginia I made two important decisions that helped to set the tone for the entire year. These two decisions were very simple. First, I decided I was going to get up every morning a minimum of two hours before I needed to be anywhere (if I had a nine o'clock class, I got up at seven). Second, I made a promise that I was not going to use the snooze bar on my alarm clock. You may laugh, but if you are like me and the idea of an early morning causes pain and despair, you will understand the incredible temptation a snooze bar presents.

These two decisions were made so as to insure that I spent time alone with God each day. Not just ten minutes of reading the Psalms, but a real time of thinking, praying, and studying the Bible. About this time our dad wrote a letter to Chris and me in which he encouraged us to make a priority of spending time in the morning with God. He shared some words of C. S. Lewis. "The moment you wake up each morning all your wishes and hopes for the day rush at you like wild animals and the first job each morning consists of shoving it all back; and listening to that other voice, taking that other point of view, letting that other larger, stronger, quieter life come flowing in." In the Psalms, David affirms this need for a time of devotion as you start the day. "In the morning, O LORD, you hear my voice; in the morning I lay my requests before you and wait in expectation" (Ps. 5:3).

"Be quiet before the Lord—learn how to or you'll go crazy!" says Amy, a recent graduate of Grand Canyon College. Like Amy, one of the biggest lessons I had learned prior to my final year was that *if I was going to survive at all as a Christian, I had to spend time alone with God.* Even on mornings when the last thing in the world I wanted to do was read my Bible, I knew I had to, not because I wanted to earn spiritual "extra credit," but for sheer spiritual survival. The great sixteenth-century reformer Martin Luther expressed the same idea when he said, "I have so much going on around me that I cannot get by without two or three hours of prayer *every day*"! I may not have had the intense discipline of Luther, but as I read and prayed that final year, I grew in my faith. Not only was I surviving as a Christian, I was beginning to fall more and more in love with the God who created me and saved me.

Even though sheer spiritual survival seems to be a pretty compelling reason to spend time with God, many students don't bother or claim they don't have the time. Why? Jim told us the simple truth: *"While the college schedule offers more free time to pursue God, it also challenges our self-discipline to do so."* Two words, one problem: self-discipline.

Remember how we said the first ten days can be the most important of your college career? These first ten days are overwhelming by anyone's standards. You are in a completely new place, surrounded by strangers, trying to figure out your schedule and most likely staying up until the wee hours of the morning every night because there is so much to do and so many people to talk to. It is the busiest free time you'll ever have. During weeks like this it is easy to abandon daily priorities and throw out all semblance of discipline. And yet for many college students this isn't just a temporary abandonment; it is the peak of a long steep slope down which they have just begun to tumble. Although it's fun and exhilarating at first, you eventually hit critical speed and lose all control.

In chapter 2 we talked about the importance of taking a stand on issues right from the very beginning. Just as important as establishing standards for conduct during the first ten days is the importance of establishing daily priorities that grow into daily habits. These disciplines then provide a foundation and direction for everything we become involved in.

Making It Happen and Sticking with It

The obvious place to start in making time alone with God a daily priority is to find a time and place in which to do it. The first thing to do is set a time in your daily schedule. The simple act of deciding when to get alone and actually writing it down is a big help. Then when people ask you to do something or you are tempted to spend time elsewhere, you can turn to your calendar and say, "Sorry, I'm already booked." We have found that having time alone with God first thing in the morning works well for most people. It is a good way to avoid the unpredictable nature of the rest of the day and countless evening activities. Some people might tell you that if you don't have your time alone with God first thing in the morning, you aren't a good Christian. It's true the Gospels often mention that Jesus would steal away early in the morning to spend time alone praying. But *what matters most is not so much the time of day but the quality of your time.* Some students suggest devoting time in the mornings to prayer, then setting aside a block of time in the afternoon for biblical study and reflection. However you schedule your time, you want to give God the best you have in everything you do, and you want to be disciplined in doing it. The trick to getting started is to *consistently spend the best time of your day with him—time when you are awake, alert, and eager to learn.*

Once you have set a time, the next piece of the puzzle is finding a place. Here is where you can be both creative and practical. My freshman year I quickly discovered that the football stadium was open and empty in the mornings. It's not a bad deal when you can have a peaceful time alone with God, and great seats on top of that. If your roommate is either very quiet or already out, your own room may also be an obvious choice. Other options might include the student lounge, the library, empty classrooms, or a campus garden. Most schools have some sort of a chapel on or near campus. These are almost always open and (sadly) just as often empty—a great place to hide. We even have some friends who found unused stairwells, elevators, hallways, or even discovered ways onto roofs of buildings to be alone with the Lord. Not that we're suggesting you scale tall buildings . . . The bottom line: *Be creative with what is convenient.* "Be with God," urges one friend. "Find secret quiet places. Develop a routine. You are in charge of your schedule."

A Matter of Integrity

Being disciplined in spending daily time with God is not just a practical issue of spiritual survival. When we think of it only in this manner, time with God quickly descends into a Christian duty that you do and then cross off your list for the day while moving on to other things. It is definitely a matter of survival, but it is also an issue of integrity and perseverance.

Perhaps you or one of your friends is a serious athlete. I had a handful of friends at college who were varsity athletes, and I was constantly amazed at how much their lives revolved around their sport. Practice, often twice a day, was the focal point of their daily schedule. Most of them were on special diets to maximize their performance and were on a weight-lifting routine in addition to practice. Their lives were fine tuned with one goal in mind—pursuing excellence in their sport. Having been given a talent by God, they displayed integrity by being disciplined in their preparation and training, so that when it came to competing, they would be at the top of their game.

We should have the same mentality toward our faith. Paul writes to the believers in Corinth, "Do you not know that in a race all the runners run, but only one gets the prize? Run in such a way as to get the prize. Everyone who competes in the games goes into strict training. They do it to get a crown that will not last; but we do it to get a crown that will last forever" (1 Cor. 9:24–25). Similarly, he writes to the Christians in Philippi, "But one thing I do: Forgetting what is behind and straining toward what is ahead, I press on toward the goal to win the prize for which God has called me heavenward in Christ Jesus" (Phil. 3:13–14). What is the prize? The crown? The goal of our lives as Christians? I think Paul says it best at the beginning of his letter to the Ephesians: "In him [Christ] we were chosen, having been predestined according to the plan of him who works out everything in conformity with the purpose of his will, in order that we, who were the first to hope in Christ, might be for *the praise of his glory*" (Eph. 1:11–12).

Our goal is to glorify God. A life lived with this in mind has a very specific focus. With the discipline of athletes we need to train our heads, hearts, and hands to live with this one goal in mind. One of the central disciplines in keeping this focus is seeking God daily and spending time alone with him. Otherwise we tend to lose focus: our motivations become muddied, our priorities fragmented, and the interlocking integrity of our lives quickly falls to pieces. We give God our full concentration not only because we need to, as a matter of survival, but because we want to, as a matter of integrity.

But what does it all look like? How is it supposed to work?

Reading, Speaking, and Listening

I remember reading a flyer on campus that advertised workshops for living "a spiritually guided life." By sitting comfortably in different positions, taking traditional medicines, maneuvering one's hands and fingers in obscure ways, and listening to the guidance of a "trained" facilitator, any average student could move through various levels of spiritual energy and attain a true "life force." Thankfully, the attention God desires from us in our times with him is a little more straightforward and a little less eccentric. Even still, it's easy for us to get off track in how we approach our time alone with God, and it is good for us to be reminded of the basics.

Reading

If we were to take a survey of what Christian college students read during their quiet times, we might become convinced that God's real name is Oswald Chambers and that the actual title of the Bible is *My Utmost for His Highest.* Okay, so it's a little bit of an exaggeration, but not much. *My Utmost for His Highest* is a great devotional book, but like any devotional guide it should be read along with, not instead of, the Bible. There is a whole industry set up to provide all kinds of quiet-time tools—workbooks, calendars, checklists . . . you name it. Some are useful, many are not. God gave us his Word, and whatever else we might use in our times with God, the Bible must be central. It is the principal means by which he has chosen to speak to us. In it God reveals his character and our character, showing us who he is, who we are, and how we might become more like him. Remember, if we sincerely want to live lives "in praise of his glory," we must learn what acceptable praise is and genuinely hunger after his glory. We do this by beginning with his Word.

In the New Testament, Paul encourages his young friend Timothy to read and trust Scripture. He says, "All Scripture is God-breathed and is useful for teaching, rebuking, correcting and training in righteousness, so that the man of God may be thoroughly equipped for every good work" (2 Tim. 3:16–17). What a great model this is for our own reading of the Bible.

First of all, the Bible will teach us. From it we learn both simple and complex truths about the world around us, about God, and about ourselves. Through it we see more clearly God's perfection and his perfect will for us.

Second, the Bible should rebuke us. As it teaches us more about God, the way he deals with his people, and our relationship with him, we naturally discover conflict between our lives and the life he desires us to live. We will be chastened and challenged to change.

Third, God's Word corrects us. Having been shown how and where we fail we are then shown how we should act and who we should become instead. God doesn't get angry or annoyed with us and then turn his back; instead he gently rebukes us and then provides a way forward by showing us the direction to take and the way we should behave.

Finally, God's Word is a tool for training. While we may not always find ourselves chastened by a passage of Scripture, we find value in reading and studying the Bible because it constantly works on us, building us up so that we may be "thoroughly equipped" for everything God has in store for us.

"I feel like every time I open the Bible . . . God reveals something to me," says Heidi. "It may not be the answer I'm looking for, and it may not even be the question I'm trying to answer, but he works on me during those times." God's Word teaches us, challenges us, corrects us, and continually builds us up, enabling us to become all that God has called us to be and so revealed in his Word.

Speaking

I know it's awful, but sometimes I find it difficult not to laugh when people are praying out loud. Have you ever *really* listened to other people, much less yourself, pray? A typical prayer often goes like this: "Father, I just pray that you, Lord, would help me as I prepare for my exam tomorrow, God; help me to study hard and do the best I can, Jesus; and Lord, just help me to pass this exam, Father, amen." Do we ever talk to our friends like this? Stream of consciousness, no periods, all commas. How often in the course of a conversation do you call someone by their name or other recognized title? Do you ask people to "just" do something as if it were no big deal to them and you deserved it anyway?

Contrast the above prayer with Jesus' prayer in Matthew 6:9–13.

> Our Father in heaven,
> hallowed be your name,
> your kingdom come,
> your will be done
> on earth as it is in heaven.
> Give us today our daily bread.
> Forgive us our debts,
> as we also have forgiven our debtors.
> And lead us not into temptation,
> but deliver us from the evil one.

How unbelievably simple! It begins with respectful recognition of God's holiness, is followed by a humble request for a basic need, is built on by seeking forgiveness, and finishes with a request for the future. There is so much to the Lord's Prayer that we dare not try to dig it all out. The important point is that Jesus preceded this prayer by saying, "This then, is how you should pray." It isn't necessarily *what* you should pray but an excellent model of *how* you should pray.

Jesus demonstrates that for us prayer is a respectful yet confident approach by a sinful creature to an almighty God. A God who, in spite of our condition, wants to hear from us, to know our thoughts and needs, and promises to respond to our requests within the perfection of his will. In one of the psalms, David cries out to God, "Search me, O God, and know my heart; test me and know my anxious thoughts. See if there is any offensive way in me, and lead me in the way everlasting" (Ps. 139:23–24). His prayer is one that finishes with a listening heart.

Listening

Have you ever dozed off while talking to a friend on the phone or while in class only to have the professor call on you? It's embarrassing, we know. Most of us are not naturally very good listeners, but perhaps the most important part of spending time alone with God is summed up in the act of listening.

Whether we are reading the Bible, memorizing a verse, consulting a Bible commentary, praying for guidance, or asking forgiveness, our overarching mission should be to listen to God. *Listening ears reveal a ready mind willing to be changed, a receptive heart ready to be molded, and open hands ready to work.* They also are a telltale sign of that noble Christian virtue humility. Psalm 139 is the cry of a broken and humble person in humility before a great God. We likewise show our humility in every aspect of our time with God by opening our ears and listening. Even when we are speaking in prayer we can listen to what we are saying while thinking about the words we choose and what we are trying to communicate. We listen closely to God as he reveals himself through

Scripture. We listen to the prompting of his Spirit in silent moments or perhaps when reflecting on a single verse. We listen to other people, through biblical discussion and Bible commentaries, in order to help us understand God and ourselves better.

Spilling Over

Good relationships rely on consistent, open communication. This is especially true of our relationship with God. *We engage with God in regular communication because it is a simple humble exercise in lordship every day.* The point is not to worship our quiet times, or pat ourselves on the back for such impressive spiritual devotion. We spend this time with God because we yearn for his input in our lives, we covet his thoughts, and we want him involved. Because this is a living and active relationship, *we should never limit our interaction with God to our daily, scheduled time alone with him.* This is only the beginning. "Every moment of life ought to reflect the changes and consolidation God is working within us," explains writer and teacher Donald Drew in his essay "Authentic Spirituality." This personal transformation only begins with the daily discipline of specific time spent alone with God. Don't be intimidated; self-discipline is not as impossible as we may think! Paul tells Timothy that "God did not give us a spirit of timidity, but a spirit of power, of love and of self-discipline" (2 Tim. 1:7). Like Timothy, we have already received the gift of self-discipline. All we have to do is choose to use it in our time with God. The attitude and focus we have during this time should then spill over into every facet of our lives as we seek to practice the presence of God moment by moment. As our thoughts turn into prayers and our focus is fixed on Christ, he becomes the single overriding passion in our lives. He will consume our hearts and minds in a way that Jane expressed when she shared with us: "I would not trade being accepted into Northwestern's film school, working alongside Steven Spielberg, going to the Oscars in the most beautiful dress in the world, starring in Kenneth Branagh's next Shakespearean film, being able to play the tin whistle with the Chieftains and winning a gold medal in foosball in the Olympics for what I've gained at college—a love relationship with Jesus Christ."

The great news is that we can all share in that love relationship with Christ; the price has been paid and the road already prepared. We only have to desire a close relationship with Christ, seek him and his Word, and let him be the guide of our lives.

Questions for Study and Reflection

Study passages: Psalm 119:9–11; 103–6

1. Why is daily time alone with God so important? What are some key elements of this time?

2. What does it mean to hide God's Word in your heart? To seek God with all your heart? How is God's Word an essential key to knowing him?

3. What is your current pattern of time alone with God? Do you want to make changes? What will they be?

4. Take some time this week to write down what you are learning in these times with the Lord and share it with a friend who would be willing to do the same thing.

THE INNER CIRCLE

Where Fellowship Begins

Dan grew up in a Christian home. Though a strong believer, early in college he began to get involved in a scene where his faith slipped out of focus and almost out of his life. That is, until his friends helped pull him out of it. This is an excerpt from a letter Dan wrote to Kevin, one of those friends.

CHAPTER 5

"I have been meaning to meet up with you to talk, but exams and such have prevented me from doing so. I have something very important to tell you, though; so I will do it over e-mail instead. . . .

"When I got up here [to college] this year, it was a world of temptation. I thought that things couldn't get any better. I could party all the time and never have to worry about getting caught or where to go when I was drunk. My best friend, Austin, was going to Campus Crusade and Fellowship of Christian Athletes, but I always made excuses as to why I couldn't go. In actuality, it was because I was ashamed. I did not want to think about God because I could see just how bad I had become. . . . I had once been so good and I had done some awful things since then. Would God even want to see me . . . ?

"In January an event took place that scared me into the stark realization that I had fallen and that things were not all right with me. . . . I remember praying on my knees literally for hours. I was prostrate on the ground, humble, hurting, crying, scared, and not sure if relief could be found through prayer or not. But I had nowhere else to go. Right then I asked God to help me rededicate my life to him.

"Austin was faithful and kept asking me to go to Crusade until one day I finally said yes. I don't know why; maybe it was to shut him up, but I tend to believe it was the Spirit. I started attending Crusade regularly, and things were getting a little better. . . .

"I did not stop drinking right away, but I had cut down a great deal. Then I went to Big Break [a Christian conference] and had a wonderful time. . . . I sure had fallen a long way, but now I knew that I could . . . turn my life around, and I did. No wait, I didn't— God did.

"When I got back I went straight to my stash . . . and threw out a total of forty beers. . . . It was an outward and visible sign of my inward rebirth. Since then things have been great. I'm not saying that everything is roses, but God is with me through it all. Right here . . . by my side holding me up. . . . I have engulfed myself in prayer and the Word and am stronger now in my faith than ever before. He has provided me with Christian fellowship and friends who love me for my heart . . . friends like you.

"I want to thank you, Kev. Thank you for your faithfulness, thank you for your love, thank you for your prayers. I needed all the help that I could get at a time when I didn't even know anything was wrong. It is people like you who have helped me to get to where I am now. You helped me start living again."

The central relationship in a Christian's life is his or her own relationship with God. But thankfully, this relationship doesn't take place in a vacuum. *It is a necessary part of our individual relationship with God that we also be in close meaningful relationships with other Christians.* As we see in Dan's letter, these relationships with other Christians often make all the difference in the world for our faith and growth as believers. We have been created with community in mind and, in a word, we need *fellowship.*

But fellowship is an overused and often misunderstood word. We talk about having good fellowship, but what does that really mean? What does good fellowship look like?

In the New Testament the word for fellowship usually signifies the idea of "commonness," or "sharing in common." Having difficulty trying to put this idea of fellowship into words, we turned to John Stott's book *One People* and discovered a wonderfully simple description of fellowship as three interrelated types of sharing. First of all, fellowship is what we *share in together,* meaning our common salvation in Jesus Christ. Second, fellowship is what we *share out together,* or our common service to the community around us in both sharing the gospel and our lives. Finally, fellowship is what we *share with one another,* our reciprocal relationships of accountability, love, and care. In this way we see that fellowship leads us to face God together in worship, face each other in mutual growth and accountability, and face the world together in love and service.

This idea of fellowship having three directions in which it points us (to God, to one another, and to others) is broader and more exciting than what most of us think of when we talk about fellowship. It suddenly takes on much greater significance than Wednesday night meetings at the university chapel, because *fellowship is not so much an act Christians participate in as it is a fact of our being together in Christ.*

Throughout the New Testament, the first Christians were called to be in fellowship with one another, sharing in, sharing out, and sharing together. The writer of Hebrews says, "Let us consider how we may spur one another on toward love and good deeds. Let us not give up meeting together, as some are in the habit of doing, but let us encourage one another—and all the more as you see the Day approaching" (Heb. 10:24–25). At the beginning of his letter to the Christians in Rome, Paul describes how he longs to come and see them so "that you and I may be mutually encouraged by each other's faith" (Rom. 1:12).

What picture do you think Paul had in mind? What would mutual encouragement look like in practice? Most likely he had something very personal, genuine, and intimate in mind. He longed for the company of fellow Christians and the time to listen to them share about God's work in their lives. He knew the value of knowing and being known, loving and being loved within the body of believers devoted to Christ. In fact, he longed for it. Any discussion of fellowship should begin by focusing not on what it looks like in a large group but on how it takes shape in the inner circle of our relationships, the place where true fellowship begins. For what each of us longs for are friendships that are powerful sources of fellowship.

Being Intentional

Many of us have written thank you letters to friends and relatives to express our gratefulness for birthday presents, Christmas presents, and so on. It is like a thoughtful receipt we write in official recognition of a gift. Dan's letter to his friend Kev is another kind of thank you note. Only we get the feeling Kev's gift is not a onetime deal but an ongoing gift of true friendship. "Thank you for your faithfulness, thank you for your love, thank you for your prayers," Dan writes. Having witnessed the power of God in transforming his life, Dan's attention is drawn sharply back to the faithfulness of Austin and Kev—two friends used by God to help him "start living again."

The best soil for growing meaningful Christian fellowship is meaningful Christian friendships. This doesn't mean you have to be singing praise songs, performing skits, and taking turns giving talks every time you go to lunch or otherwise interact with your friends—thus mingling fellowship events with friendship events in an awkward way. Instead, recall that fellowship is anchored in *the fact of our being together in Christ.* Most of us tend to think of friendships *and* fellowship as occasionally overlapping areas of day-to-day life, but in this chapter we want to deliberately think of fellowship within the context of friendship before moving on in the next chapter to talk about fellowship in the larger group. To bring fellowship and friendship together we need to be intentional.

God did not craft us to be independent, isolated followers who have to tough things out on our own. Were that the case, college would be an intolerably lonely place. Instead, he designed in us doorways for sharing with one another and being joined together in Christ. He has given us the gift of having close friends and being a close friend to others. Jeanne, a graduate of the University of Richmond, reflected on the value of clinging to close Christian friends who "spurred me on and encouraged me." She went on to say that "sharing life can be hard and it can be a risk, but my faith grew only as I shared it and lived it." The task of facing basic but difficult questions such as "How does my faith impact the things I do?" and "How do God's purposes for me bear on this decision?" was made more manageable by turning to the fellowship of her close friends.

Now, for Jeanne, and for nearly everyone else we spoke with, such Christian friendships were not exactly waiting for her as soon as she showed up at college. Another friend, Kristen, made this point clearly while speaking to a group of high school seniors. "It's important to remember that it takes a long time to become friends with people, especially good friends. I think many people expect to make the best friends of their life within the first month of college and are very upset when they still don't feel like they know people and no one is like their best friend from high school. It usually takes longer than we expect."

So have realistic expectations. Friendships are not found. They are built over time and with great effort. But also have clear ambitions to take the naturally forming friendships you do have and see them transformed into powerful centers of fellowship. To go a step beyond the average friendship let's look at three different types of *intentional friendship,* all of which show how an existing relationship can become more purposeful and directed by God. Few students we spoke with could say they had these types of relationships every week of every year of their college experience, but when such friendships were developed they were appreciated and maintained with great care. Why? Because all three are fixed firmly in the bottom-line goal of *being purposefully united in a fellowship relationship directed by God for his glory.*

Accountability

Earlier in the book we mentioned our friend Brian, who was somewhat disappointed with the unexpected realities of "Christian" life at his small Southern California college. Things began to improve for Brian when he became intentional in friendships shared with a few other guys. As he told us, "I had four really close friends, and we fed each other. We treated each other as though we were on a journey together. . . . We were connected and growing together. We challenged and sharpened each other like iron on iron. We moved from being know-it-all Christians to know-nothing faithful followers of Christ. We became less self-centered. We thought of the implications of being Christians first, then looked at how that ought to affect our role in other things." *A friendship with a purpose of accountability is one where those involved regularly encourage one another to integrate their faith in all areas of their life.* This is iron on iron—a consistent, Christ-centered sharpening of one another. The reality of shared lordship makes this possible, while the goal of integrity in our lives makes it crucial.

Brian and his friends began to ask themselves and each other how their faith in Christ should lead them in their thinking and behavior. They became intentional in accountability during their second semester in college and remain so to this day as recent college graduates. Whether it is a group like his or a one-on-one friendship, the point is to be asking one another tough but loving questions about how your faith is being lived out each day. This often works best with a very small group of friends—people who are interested in sharing together about struggles or about things being learned in each other's daily times alone with God. In his letter, Dan mentioned that he "needed all the help that I could get at a time when I didn't even know anything was wrong." What he needed, and what we frequently do know we need, is someone to ask us about the decisions we are making, how we are handling temptations, and where God is fitting into each day.

This can obviously be very humbling. After all, we would much prefer to keep our weaknesses and sinful habits to ourselves. But remember, it is humbling for both parties involved. Picture two friends getting on their knees together before the Lord and asking him to use them in each other's lives for the sake of clinging to him as lord each day. That is the core of accountability. Without such accountability it is all too easy to leave God in a compartment and slip into the lifestyle changes available on a college campus. Sharpening one another can be painful and embarrassing, but when it is for the greater purpose of God's glory, it is a thing for which we are grateful. Maybe you can think of someone you would enjoy growing together with in this way. All it takes is saying, "Hey, I don't have it all together and could really enjoy growing in my faith through some intentional accountability. I wonder if you would pray about joining me in seeking the Lord through accountability together." Be deliberate about setting up a regular time to meet and talk, and go from there. Time together should be a priority. It shouldn't be based on convenience but a firm commitment to be together in faith.

Discipleship

Thad says one of the greatest spiritual experiences he had at college was the time he spent in friendship and discipleship with an older student named Andrew. "I met Andrew during my freshman year, and God immediately began to work in both our lives. Andrew took on the role of an informal discipler during my early years. . . . Every opportunity I got to spend time with this man of God exploding with excitement for the pursuit of Christ consisted of twenty questions on my part. The lessons I learned from our discussions together about Christ and life have proved to be invaluable to me."

A friendship with the purpose of discipleship is one in which a younger student meets regularly with someone who is older and more mature in the faith, for the sake of biblical study, discussion, and growth. It might be an older student, like Andrew, a fellowship group staff worker, or someone known through a nearby church that you see as a person with whom you could grow in the faith. He or she doesn't have to be a spiritual superhero but ought to be someone in whom you see a clear model of lordship, integrity, and servanthood. There are many ways this kind of friendship can work. Thankfully, God has made discipleship a natural and comfortable outgrowth of friendship. It can be routine and formal, or informal yet purposeful.

What made Thad's friendship with Andrew work was not only Thad's hunger to be discipled but Andrew's commitment to spending strategic time with someone younger in years and spiritual maturity. The fact that God blessed and used the natural friendship between the two shows us something further. Thad went on to tell us how after two years of informal discipleship, he could begin to see ways in which Andrew's personality and character had rubbed off on him. Isn't that how Christ impacted and sharpened his disciples? *Discipleship is a way of allowing the Christlikeness of an older person to leave a lasting imprint of Christlikeness on a younger person.* Paul and Timothy had a discipleship relationship. Instruction, encouragement, faithfulness, and enthusiasm for the Lord should all be ingredients of this kind of fellowship. We also will often find accountability within a discipleship relationship.

Sometimes discipleship will flow out of being involved in a small group Bible study with an older leader. We say "flow out" because being in a Bible study is not necessarily the same thing as being discipled, but it is a wonderful starting point. What would the difference be? As is modeled in Thad and Andrew's friendship, there is a need for spending deliberate time together. Maybe your Bible study leader would be willing to get together with you once a month outside of the Bible study to hang out and talk about things ranging from what's going on in your life to how the Scripture you are studying is teaching you and affecting you. There is no perfect formula for discipleship. But like accountability, if we pray for a discipleship relationship and then offer God our initiative, he will open the door in his own faithful way.

Jeanne told us that some of the most important advice she gives younger students is three words: Disciple; be discipled.

Mentoring

During her college years, Becky met regularly with a woman named Joan. Becky describes her as being "so much wiser than me" and says that "she always gave me a clear perspective on things. She fueled my flame with her descriptions of God's grace and love. . . . Every time I met her for breakfast, I left completely on fire for the rest of the day."

A friendship with the purpose of mentoring occurs when we meet regularly with an older adult who shares not only a love for God but other, often professional, interests similar to ours. While this kind of fellowship can play out in many ways, it is often the most overlooked opportunity for friendship. Many people speak of mentors in the secular sense—people who have had an important influence in academics, in a career, and so on. But, as Christians, we can form a mentoring relationship that sharpens us in similar ways and is rooted in Christ. It can be similar to an informal discipleship relationship, though we have the additional gift of seeing Christlikeness modeled by someone who is in their thirties or forties, married, maybe a parent, and interested in our professional ambitions, as well as gifts and everyday concerns.

Sure, we're dealing with people who might be our parents' age, but friendships with older mentors are surprisingly meaningful and helpful as we seek to manifest lordship, integrity, and servanthood in our lives. Of the three friendships we describe here, a mentoring relationship is the one usually requiring the most initiative on your part. Accountability and discipleship can grow more easily out of friendships you have already cultivated, but on a college campus we spend less time interacting day in and day out with potential mentors. Nevertheless, don't be discouraged. An obvious place to begin is in prayer. If it is a desire of your heart to have fellowship of this kind, it is likely God will provide. Local churches are full of adults who are hungry to serve the Lord as mentors to students. If your school has a graduate student population, there will be older Christian students there as well. College fellowship groups often have full-time staff workers who may be willing to join you in this kind of friendship or could easily connect you with an adult Christian friend of theirs.

We can both attest to the fact that God is a God who loves to connect his people, even when it seems unlikely. The important thing is to begin with a prayerful desire.

Learning the Lesson

We have taken time to discuss these three forms of Christian friendship, not to give a precise mandate for how to organize your spiritual social life but to encourage you in thinking and praying about ways in which real fellowship can manifest itself in real friendships. Accountability, discipleship, and mentoring are practical examples of what a fellowship-centered friendship can look like, a friendship that shares in, shares out, and shares with one another. If after your first semester you've found an accountability partner but haven't had any luck in being discipled or mentored, it doesn't mean you are falling short on some kind of checklist. What matters most is that you have caught the vision for making your inner circle of relationships at college a place where you are joined together with close friends in the fellowship of Christ. As simple as that may sound, we have devoted a whole chapter to this understanding of fellowship because time after time students miss the boat. Fellowship becomes that thing we do once a week with a large group of people, while friendships are those things we slowly end up in and eventually keep up with. Wrong.

Consider the critical observations of one freshman when he reflected on his experience in a large Christian organization. "It seemed like everyone loved Jesus, didn't have any problems, and was perfectly happy. I knew I didn't have it all together; how could all these people? There is a fault among Christians of not actively being real with each other. We should draw strength from each other. . . . There is a real need for sharing burdens and praying for each other." He was making a basic observation—we need each other and the fellowship of real friendships, not just social interaction built on something we share in common. Fellowship without friendship turns into a stagnate shallow pool.

A student at the end of her junior year shared how difficult her first two years had been without real fellowship. "I struggled in not having fellowship those first two years. . . . But the difference in my first two years and this year is that this year I found meaningful friendships." Not that there weren't innumerable Christian organizations available to her those first two years. Perhaps she had made the same observations as our freshman friend and was simply too frustrated to pursue more intimate fellowship. What happened? She found fellowship through meaningful Christian friendships.

There is a richness to being together in Christ that early Christians eagerly pursued and that we today may likewise enjoy. No one, to our knowledge, has ever regretted a meaningful Christian friendship. Accountability, discipleship, and mentoring are relationships that grow out of our devotion to God and to one another. In friendships such as these we find the rich soil of Christ-centered community and priceless fellowship.

Be warned, these relationships are difficult! It can be hard to find the right mentor, and it is sometimes difficult to get comfortable in an accountability relationship. We will often put older people on a pedestal and expect more from them than they are able to give, and the same will be true of others' expectations for us. Keeping these difficulties in mind, press on! These relationships are the ones that will last a lifetime.

A Vision for Times to Come

During my first year of college I got involved in a fellowship group for freshmen. I really enjoyed it but struggled with the fact that I wasn't getting to know upperclassmen very well. I saw older guys whom I admired but who naturally intimidated me. I felt unable to approach them, in spite of wanting to get to know them. One afternoon, completely out of the blue, some of these guys called me and my roommate, Jason. A group of them were driving out to a big barbecue restaurant forty-five minutes away and wanted to see if we would go with them. Why a group of senior guys wanted to hang out with us was beyond our understanding, but we jumped at the opportunity. We had a great time and enjoyed becoming friends with guys we had previously respected from a distance.

What a simple thing for them to do, and what a meaningful experience for us. In the weeks that followed, as I thought more about that evening, I realized how much I respected the guys that were even only a year ahead of me. In their own eyes they probably didn't see me as very different from themselves, but in my eyes they were leagues ahead of me. It occurred to me that in a very short time I would be in their position—I would have the great opportunity as an upperclassman to reach out in easy yet meaningful ways to younger students.

This chapter has focused on different types of friendship where fellowship takes place. We've purposefully talked about friendships where *our own growth* in Christ is a focus. And for each friendship to happen it's clear that there must be another person, often older, *pouring into* our lives. But what about relationships where the growth and encouragement of *another person* is our primary focus? What happens when we become the older student and a freshman friend of ours, having read this same chapter, wants us to disciple them?! This is the vision for times to come.

Whether we like it or not, younger people look up to us to set an example, our peers look to us to be an encouragement, and our elders, who have invested their lives in ours, look to us to prove faithful. Whether or not a younger student asks me to meet up with him regularly to encourage him in his faith, I am still responsible for being a credible witness and bearing timely instruction to the whole body of Christ. At all times and in all places, we are to be witnesses, bearing testimony to the truth of the gospel through our actions and words. When we do this, we play our part in making fellowship a living and active part of daily life for ourselves and for our closest friends.

Questions for Study and Reflection

Study passage: Colossians 3:12–17

1. The Bible is full of faithful friends who are thankful for one another. Who do you especially appreciate for encouraging and challenging you in your faith? Specifically, how have they done this?

2. Do you have someone to hold you accountable for your spiritual growth? If not, who could become your accountability partner?

3. What is the difference between pursuing growth in your faith and simply maintaining your faith? How do these two different attitudes manifest themselves in your inner-circle relationships?

4. Who are you being intentional in caring for? Who can you reach out to? How? What sort of an example do you set for those around you?

5. What does it mean to "teach and admonish one another"? How do lordship, integrity, and servanthood relate to this part of friendship?

CHRISTIAN COMMUNITY

The Body at Large

CHAPTER

6

The *News and Observer,* a newspaper many North Carolina residents find on their doorstep every day, featured a story not long ago describing the nature of campus fellowship groups at area colleges.

"Providing a home away from home is one of the key goals of most campus religious organizations, according to area campus ministers. Students from virtually every religious background can find somewhere at their school to worship, eat a meal and join in fellowship with other students" (17 October 1997).

When the secular news media features fellowship among college students, it should get our attention. Thankfully, many of the students we talked with didn't just read about fellowship in the paper—they found it.

Large or small, public or private, every college has some sort of organized Christian fellowship group. It might be run by students, by a local church, or by a national organization that planted the group on campus. Either way, it's there. The trick is to look for it. On some campuses it may be harder to find than on others, but with a little investigative zeal, a commitment to finding it, and realistic expectations, you should manage to track down a Christian organization at school—even if there's only one other person involved!

Having spent the previous chapter emphasizing the importance of developing strong friendships with a small number of other Christians, we now turn our focus to the bigger picture—the importance of having interaction with the larger body of believers on your campus. We have found it is indispensable that people get involved in large fellowship groups. Freshmen students who know this and make a point to do it are already on top of the game. At the end of her freshman year, Charlotte knew firsthand what we are talking about and urged other students to "*definitely* find a Christian organization and plug into it. Have faith that the Lord will put you where he wants you. . . . This is an incredible way to meet other strong Christians who not only will help you grow in the Lord but will enable you to see more of God by watching how he works in their lives." Why is this important if we are already sharing in, sharing out, and sharing together in our other relationships?

First of all, from a purely practical perspective, it is usually through involvement in a large fellowship group that one meets and gets to know those people who become their close friends and confidantes. Without this outlet for the whole community to gather together, it is difficult to meet one another. During the first week of classes, fellowship groups might sponsor welcoming picnics and parties on campus that are an easy first step to getting plugged in—and getting some free food along the way.

Second, we meet together in large groups because it is here that we often get the best biblical teaching on the Christian life. Though small group Bible study is a good and popular form of fellowship, we all need the enhancement of outside teaching fed into our lives.

Third, meeting with the larger community of Christians gives us a broader understanding of the body of Christ. Following on this model of the body, we come to realize that we need one another and that we are many parts. If we stay in our little circle of friendships with people very similar to us, we will never come to understand and appreciate the great diversity of the body of Christ.

Fourth, coming together as a large group is a wonderful time to enjoy corporate worship together. A time to "share in" the goodness of God.

And finally, large groups are often the best providers of dynamic opportunities to "share out" in the community and serve with compassion and generosity those who are around us.

Finding the Fellowship Fit

At small schools in small towns, it may be very clear which Christian organization you get involved in, as there may, indeed, be only one. This in many ways makes life easy—you just go. The same might be said for Christian schools where chapel or other weekly meetings are often mandatory. For those going to larger public schools, however, there is frequently a generous assortment of different Christian organizations one could be involved in. No matter where we find ourselves, with many choices or only one, we will likely face the question: What should my mindset be in getting involved with the right Christian fellowship organization?

When I arrived at college I had a good idea of what organization I would be involved in. I had older friends and an older sister who were a great help in guiding me through the maze of twenty-one Christian groups on campus. I ended up going to meetings of a well-known national organization and spent four years being actively involved. Why did I go? Older friends directed me there, saying it was a good, solid group. I felt comfortable there. I liked the other students I met. I saw that we would receive good, Bible-based teaching every week. In addition to these positives it simply felt right, not perfect by any means but somewhere I could see myself getting involved.

Now, although we would recommend getting involved in a well-known Christian group like Campus Crusade, InterVarsity, Young Life, Fellowship of Christian Athletes, or the many others that are out there, we recognize that this isn't for everyone. These are particularly good groups because they are internationally recognized; leaders and staff workers are well trained, and they are held accountable to regional directors. But on different campuses, organizations have distinct personalities, and you may feel like you couldn't possibly fit in to one of these groups. If there are other opportunities for group fellowship, investigate them. This could mean being involved at a local church or a smaller denominational fellowship organization on campus. "Take a little time to check out the lay of the land, but don't be afraid to get involved and commit to a fellowship group," says Heather.

If Christian groups are limited, and after scouting out the territory you can't find one that fits you perfectly, don't simply give up. *At this point you find the one that is closest to what you want and get involved regardless of the imperfections.* After all, there's no such thing as a group where every student thinks it's perfect. Sean might like the singing but get annoyed with the excessive group sharing times. Amy might love the sense of family in the sharing but not really get much out of the singing. Every group has its own quirks because every group has a bunch of quirky personalities within it. And yes, it can also take time to get to know and feel comfortable with the other students there. As our sister Susy so succinctly put it, "Don't be a fellowship group snob! Be willing to go and be the person no one knows." Building relationships with people and feeling welcomed into a community of fellow Christians always takes time and even work. This is a part of being in fellowship. It is important enough to warrant a little struggling along the way if things aren't great at first. Stick with it and you may be amazed at how much you learn, grow, and come to love the people you are with.

For me, involvement with a large group gave me a growing sense of Christian family by my sophomore and junior years. On Thursday evenings I would finish work on the editorial page of the student newspaper, where feeling like a stranger in the world was a daily reality, and journey across to the old chapel on campus where my Christian group met. When I got there it always felt like I was returning to the warmth of true family. The fellowship of a large group of brothers and sisters was a tremendous gift of security and encouragement.

Sadly, many students never get to enjoy that kind of community. One reason is that opportunities for good fellowship might be few and far between. A second, and more common, reason is that students often suffer from the "what does it do for me?" syndrome. We are all guilty of slipping into this somewhere along the way. One of the first symptoms of the syndrome is complaining about fellowship, especially what we don't get out of the gatherings. For example, Sean might say that he just doesn't "get a whole lot out of the sharing." Eventually this becomes like a rock in his shoe that finally frustrates him to the point that, instead of dealing with the rock, he chucks the shoe away and just quits going to the group. *He's cut himself off from a rich source of fellowship because he let a small frustration become a selfish distraction.*

It's easy for any of us to get this moviegoer mentality about fellowship. We go, we leave, and we try to decide if we would see it again. We treat fellowship like a consumer item. Unless we feel that something about the group really is not consistent with what we believe true fellowship must be, then chances are good we've got a case of "what does it do for me?" syndrome. In contrast to this, *the students who have the best experience with Christian student organizations are those who are more concerned with "giving in" than "getting out."* They realize that fellowship is larger than themselves and that by actively participating they are serving and joining a community that celebrates together the lordship of Christ.

With all this talk about fellowship groups it might seem that going to church is a duty left behind with the high school years. Actually, that could not be farther from the truth. *It is just as important to get to a good church on Sundays as it is to get to a fellowship group during the week.* If a large fellowship group is a more complete picture of the body of Christ than a small group of friends, then church is even more complete. It is good to stay in the wider body, especially appreciating the contributions of various age groups. Church is also a place to hear good teaching on a regular basis, and it is an important discipline to establish for the future, once you are out of college and away from student fellowship groups that cater to your age and location. Make church a priority. "It takes a conscious decision sometimes," says Becky. "When you go to bed Saturday night, know you are going to church Sunday morning."

Healthy Community or Insulated Sect?

 My very first night at college, our suite of ten guys went to dinner together. We had no idea where anything was, so we followed our resident advisor like sheep behind a shepherd. Although we felt pretty stupid having to be led around, there was excitement at just being there. I became friends right away with a guy named Julian. We sat across from each other at dinner, and I couldn't believe it when he bowed his head to pray. What an amazing thing. Not only did I click right away with someone in my suite, he was a Christian too! Maybe he would prove an outlet for good fellowship?

Julian was indeed a fellow believer, and we did get along, most of the time. He had a great sense of humor and an ability to turn every situation into fun. I liked having a crazy friend who was also a Christian. As the weeks went by, however, we realized that we were coming from vastly different backgrounds and had very different understandings of how faith worked itself out in daily life. It soon became clear that although Julian was a Christian, he was a different kind of Christian than I was.

Not knowing how to deal with someone who didn't quite fit my mold of what a good Christian should be, I began to distance myself. I dove headfirst into the Christian community surrounding my fellowship group, while he stayed behind. And as I built up my circle of "Christian" friends, he didn't make the cuts.

Not knowing how to integrate the different types of friends I had, I simply let relationships fall into their own categories, such as people I lived with, non-Christian friends, and Christian friends. Without meaning to I created multiple relational worlds that I crossed in and out of with no interaction between them. Friends from one group didn't know friends from another, and I did nothing to try to bring them together.

While insulating myself in the fellowship community, I was creating gaps that would later turn into unbridgeable chasms. The basic problem was that I was judging people. It never felt like I was judging them, but by the simple act of separating them in my head, I deemed one group "worthy" and the other "necessary extras."

What I was doing on a personal level, many of us often do on a corporate level with our involvement in large fellowship groups. I was finding my identity in the group I had gotten involved in, and I had no sense that I needed to integrate the different parts of my life. I figured compartmentalization was the easiest and most efficient way of doing things. I couldn't have been more wrong. Part of the problem was that I didn't know any better.

Let's backtrack for a minute. Many of us, when we first arrive at college, are in need of a strong dose of Christian fellowship and feeding. Whatever our backgrounds may be, we are now in an atmosphere where there is good fellowship, and we want to enjoy it. Thus we spend the first several months or even the first year of school getting heavily involved in "Christian" activities. From small groups to large groups, retreats, summer projects, accountability partners, and church on Sunday, we feast on the opportunities presented to us.

The irony is that strong fellowship groups can easily go too far by insulating the students involved and creating a subculture. "A major problem I have seen," says Scotty, "is the separation of the Christian community from the rest of the student body. By this I mean the tendency of Christians, once in a fellowship group, to never step outside of it, to be so busy with retreats and events and hanging out with their fellow believers, where things are comfortable, that friendships with those who need Christ go largely ignored and undeveloped." *Nearly every Christian student we talked to who had been at a school with excellent opportunities for fellowship saw the separatism of Christian students from the rest of the student body as a major problem.* While these subcultures can be an incredible source of life and strength, they can, at the same time, become a slow-working poison.

As we get more and more deeply involved in the Christian subculture, our friendships with non-Christians may begin to slip away. We don't know our hallmates because we're never home. We see class only as an academic exercise where we need to be faithful students, not a place where we could conceivably learn something or build relationships with other students. When this happens and you lose all contact with the world of college beyond the borders of your tight-knit community, you have ceased being a healthy community and become more like an insulated sect. Additionally, as we grow and mature in our faith, understanding how strongly it urges us to be in the world and not of it, we come to realize that in our seeking not to be *of* the world, we have accidentally ceased to be *in* it as well. At this point, integrity has officially left the building.

This is where we all need to hear the advice of Chris's roommate, Damon. "Become involved but not confined. Become active in the Christian community. Surround yourself with good people. However, do not confine yourself to the Christian community."

Subverting the Subculture

Now that we've made you sufficiently paranoid, let's try to examine how the problems might be avoided. How can you tell if you're in a subculture or just enjoying very good group fellowship? Here are a few useful signs that might suggest you are a bit too separated.

1. You don't have any close non-Christian friends.
2. The people on your hall hang out together, but you never take part.
3. Your "Christian" activities far outnumber all other activities combined.
4. You hang out separately with your Christian and non-Christian friends, creating two distinct circles of relationships.
5. You are no longer friends with people you genuinely liked at the beginning of school but haven't had time for since.
6. The people you live with don't know your Christian friends and vice versa.
7. You say no to non-Christian friends because you have already said yes to Christian friends.
8. Activities have become more important than relationships.
9. Your academic life has taken on secondary, even tertiary, importance.
10. You are doing "Christian" things most nights of the week.

The list could go on, but we think you see the point. Thomas observed these shortcomings so vividly at the University of Colorado that he had to bluntly remind himself and his friends that "we as believers must not completely separate ourselves from the world around us!" Obviously we all agree with that, but in practice we have a track record of failure. So how do we overcome these tendencies and prevent them in the first place?

The first step to take in trying to sort out a situation like this and overcome the tendency to subculturize is to see what the roots of the problem are. The roots, to us, seem to be in a misplaced focus of our faith, a misled sense of dualism, and a completely missing search for integrity.

It is wonderful to be part of a strong Christian community. Living a godly life and growing in faith become much more tangible when we are surrounded by other faithful people who encourage and challenge us. Over time, however, some of us come to depend more heavily on the stability provided for our faith by the group than on the dynamic strength of a personal relationship with Christ. *The first root problem of an insulated subculture is that instead of having Christ at the center of our lives, we have Christian community at the center.*

A friend who saw these very things happening among Christians at her school warned other students that "fellowship and accountability are key ingredients to a good Christian faith. However, those keys can quickly lead to your downfall if you associate your relationship with Christ with the people around you." Another student, recognizing the same problem at a different school, said, "Don't mistake lots of Christian fellowship and activities for a healthy relationship with Christ. It's subtle and easy to do, but Christ must come first, personally, before 'corporateness' can be meaningful and worthwhile."

When community becomes your primary source of comfort, strength, and faith, instead of Christ himself, you are in a state of unhealthy dependency. Community is a necessary and God-given component of our faith, and in a sense we are created to be codependent creatures all functioning together as different parts of the body of Christ. But be careful that you do not put your faith in the body. Our faith is in Christ, who then assigns us our place in the body and gives us the gifts to fulfill our role as unique contributors within the fellowship of believers. Because of this, Christ must come before community, and Christian community can be found only under Christ.

A second possible root of the separated Christian subculture is a dualistic way of thinking that divides everything up into sacred and secular categories. Seeing things from this perspective leads to compartmentalization. We see friends as either Christian or non-Christian, activities as either Christian or non-Christian, professors as either friendly to Christians or anti-Christian. In this way we subtly judge everything we see and do. We naturally want more and more of the sacred in our lives and less of the secular, so we unthinkingly begin to associate less with non-Christian friends, drop out of non-Christian groups, and take classes only from Christian-friendly professors.

When someone thinks and acts like this, she reveals that she has lost all desire to search for integrity. This mindset lazily categorizes people, places, and activities without seeing in all of them the potential for God's redemptive work.

All things should be done to God's glory. If they can't, then we shouldn't be doing them, period. If we see all situations as opportunities for redemption, instead of categorizing them as Christian or non-Christian, we will be more integrated, more daring, and more free with our faith. Rather than seeing a class taught by a professor who is anti-Christian as something to avoid, why not take the class and get to know the professor, seeing him on his office hours, building a relationship with him, learning from him, and maybe even sharing your ideas with him!? Why not join the university singing group rather than the Christian one? You still glorify God by using your gifts, and you are a redemptive presence in an otherwise godless place. If drinking is not a temptation for you, why not get a Christian friend and go to the fraternity party you've been invited to? (Note: it is important to do these things with another Christian for mutual support.) Some people may be too drunk even to carry on a conversation, but who knows who might be hurting and need a sober, godly person to talk to. Andrew felt God wanted him to have a presence at a fraternity known more for its parties and drinking than anything else. He suffered through the trials and frustrations of fraternity initiation and eventually won respect from the brothers for his faith. Steadily, he worked to develop meaningful relationships with the brothers and sparked a lot of conversation about the Lord. He was eventually named social chair, of all things. The parties just aren't what they used to be.

If we are deliberately putting our faith in Christ, setting aside dualistic ways of thinking, and actively pursuing a fully integrated life under the lordship of Christ, we will go a long way toward avoiding the separatist Christian subcultures that exist on so many campuses across the country. We will enjoy the wonderful gift of participating in the body of Christ on campus while actively building bridges that draw others to the richness of Christian fellowship.

Unity as Witness

Just as divisions arise between Christian and non-Christian campus cultures, fractures can occur within the Christian community itself. The body of Christ often starts to fragment and split across lines of denomination, worship style, or race. Some forms of fragmentation are natural, but others are hurtful, and when non-Christians observe it from the outside, it looks even uglier.

One campus newspaper at a large public school ran an editorial cartoon portraying Christian disunity on campus. The cartoon depicted a freshman being pulled on his left arm by one campus Christian group and on his right arm by another Christian group. Perceived as rivals, the two groups were supposedly fighting over who could recruit this new freshman into their circle. The caption read "Campus Holy Wars." Ouch! It was a brutal shot at both groups, and though not wholly accurate, it had a bit of truth to it. Leaders from both groups promptly wrote a letter to the editor together, in which they denied such hostile opposition and affirmed each other's work toward the greater goal of serving Christ on campus. But the statement had been made, and the perception of ugly disunity was clearly there.

A major source of Christian fragmentation on campuses is in the sensitive area of race. Sadly, many campuses have Christian organizations that are often unconsciously segregated by race or ethnic group. Groups are predominantly white, black, or Asian, with little mixing. There may not be any bad feelings between the groups, but the mere fact of separation shows complacence and can be hurtful. With race being the major source of tension and conflict that it is on campuses, Christian students need to be concerned. First, there is a clear biblical imperative for reconciliation and unity. Second, this is a huge opportunity for Christian students to demonstrate to their campuses what true Christian unity looks like.

At the University of Virginia, the Lord laid this issue on the hearts of a few students, and they responded. Like many universities, UVA had an atmosphere of racial strife. As a minority, black students had their own community, and as a majority, white students had theirs. With a few exceptions, meaningful racial interaction was scarce. In the dining halls, for example, white students sat in one section and black students sat in another—crossing over just didn't happen. Informal segregation was a fact of student life. University officials and various student organizations tried to combat the problem through dialogues and activities, but nothing came of it. To make things worse, Christian fellowship groups were also split along racial lines.

Feeling the burden to engage this hard reality, a small pocket of students began to meet and pray together. They were a racially mixed group, and through praying together they began to see the value of simply building relationships with one another—of knowing each other and understanding one another's worlds on campus. Soon these relationships gained momentum and more relationships began to develop. We'll let one of these students, Christy, share her personal reflections on the experience.

"Our desire was to bring black and white Christians together, not only for the purpose of racial healing but so that we could be a witness to the rest of the unbelieving community at school. I had attended several racial dialogues and left with the feeling that nothing had really been accomplished. Realizing that any sort of coming together as a group had to begin at an individual level, I began singing with Black Voices, a black gospel choir and student fellowship. (I love gospel music!) Walking in the first time was hard. I was nervous and wondered if members judged my motives for being there. As I continued to attend, however, I slowly began to build friendships and even found a girl who would become my new housemate, Kim!

"As our little group continued to meet and pray each week, relationships grew stronger and more students were drawn into the vision. Spring break was approaching and a new idea came up. With the developing interest in unity, we thought it would be important to have a context in which to act upon our common vision. What better way than to get away for a week with other brothers and sisters in Christ and serve in a missions capacity? Thirty-five students, black and white, went, and it proved to be a life-changing experience for the entire group."

The trip's momentum carried back onto campus. The vision was growing. A joint worship service was held, where previously divided Christian groups of different races came together for a night of fellowship. A talk was given on the need for reconciliation among the body of Christ. "People poured in until the auditorium overflowed," said Christy. "The Spirit of the Lord was truly present." Additional steps were taken, and students continued to meet and pray together weekly. The color line in the dining hall was broken for the first time as a group of black and white students shared a table together amid the glares and head-shaking of other students. The campus simply did not know how to respond. "What began with a few committed students praying for unity among the body of Christ turned into a wave of acknowledgment and support for Christian unity throughout the school."

It is challenging, but the call to true unity among Christian students can lead to amazing things. When students trust the Lord and take a few bold steps together, it sends a message that is undeniable and powerful, breaking beyond the body of Christ and engaging with the world around us.

Questions for Study and Reflection

Study passages: Acts 2:42–47; 1 Peter 4:7–11

1. What steps will you take to find a Christian fellowship group this year at college? If you have a choice, how might you decide which one to join?

2. How can you use your gifts and special talents to encourage others in your group?

3. How will you find a church that you want to be involved with? What are the marks of a living church as described in Acts?

4. What can you do to bring your Christian and non-Christian friends together?

5. On your own or with a small group, pray for God to give you a vision for impacting your school.

EVANGELISM: SHARING IT OUT

The Pit of Despair

On my campus, we were visited about once a month by a middle-aged Christian man whom students referred to as the Pit Preacher. He would stand in the center of campus in an area known as the Pit and spend the afternoon preaching his version of the message of Christ to any and all who would listen. He would shout criticisms of the "sinful living" rampant among college students, thump his Bible in angry dramatic fashion, and warn students of the fires of hell that awaited them if they did not repent and turn. He considered himself an evangelist. He was not a well-liked man.

Evangelism is a word that gets everyone's blood boiling. Few other words in the Christian vocabulary have the ability to fill us either with excitement or absolute dread. It rings of obligation for some, of opportunity for others. It can take the shape of an activity on your weekly calendar, or you can do it all the time without even thinking about it. Some people are naturally gifted at it, while many of us find the idea of evangelizing someone terrifying, even a bit distasteful. Why is this? Most likely those of us who are scared by evangelism have always thought of it in the wrong way.

So what is evangelism anyway? The straightforward way of defining it is that it is the act of sharing Jesus with people who don't know him. It is spreading the good news of the life, death, and resurrection of Jesus Christ. In the previous chapter we explained the importance of not becoming "too Christian"—of not being confined to the Christian community and neglecting the rest of your campus. As we go on to discuss evangelism in this chapter, we have the rest of your campus first and foremost in mind. We want to look at how this idea of evangelism works as the sharing out of our faith.

Why bother? If our lives have truly been transformed by the good news of Jesus Christ, we shouldn't even have to ask this question. We share Christ first because we love God and second because we love people. Because we live under the *lordship* of God, we will desire whatever he desires. He "wants all men to be saved and to come to a knowledge of the truth" (1 Tim. 2:4). So do we. We also share Christ because our love for people compels us to as we desire that they might have eternal life. This is yet another facet of *servanthood,* by which we refuse to keep for ourselves a treasure and a joy that is meant for others to enjoy as well.

The Word Became Flesh

Most of us become Christians as a result of the influence of some person in our life, perhaps a good friend or family member. Think about the characteristics of the person who helped you to come to faith in Christ. They got to know you, loved you for who you were, shared their life with you, and eventually shared with you about Christ. They never hid their faith from you; it was such a natural part of who they were that when it was appropriate it never seemed strange for them to talk about it. Maybe you had a sudden conversion experience, or maybe it happened gradually over time and you aren't really sure when you became a Christian. Regardless of how it all happened, there was most likely a person in your life who made all the difference. The secret to evangelism is remembering that you simply have to be that person for other people.

John's Gospel begins with a mysteriously poetic introduction to the life of Christ: *"The Word became flesh* and made his dwelling among us. We have seen his glory, the glory of the One and Only, who came from the Father, full of grace and truth" (John 1:14). "The Word became flesh." Have you ever thought about what that might mean? The good news of God for the salvation of all humankind was not something that could simply be stated. It required the living, breathing presence of a transcendent God. The Word had to become flesh in order for God's redemptive plan to come to fruition. He had to die for us and be raised from the dead in order that there might be good news.

In the same way, sharing our faith with others requires both words and deeds, or if you like polysyllabic words, both proclamation and demonstration. We must share not only the Word of God but also the flesh of God—a demonstration of the truth of the gospel through the way we live. Our actions and words must speak together. *Just as Christ couldn't simply proclaim redemption without being sacrificed for us, we can't simply proclaim God's Word without living it out.*

But what exactly is it that we want people to see in us? Let's look back at the verse. When Jesus came, he came in "glory," "full of grace and truth." *The way we live should point to a greater glory beyond us by being full of grace and firm in the truth.*

We should be people full of grace, reflections of the grace brought by Christ. Grace is the receiving of a gift you don't deserve. We are filled with grace when we accept salvation as a free gift from God. So we are first filled with grace, and once filled we share it with others. But what does this look like? To treat another person with grace is to see in them the image of God, to focus on their creation in the image of God rather than on the tarnish that has covered it, and to lovingly lead them to discover the ultimate grace come in the form of the person of Jesus Christ. This means being patient, nonjudgmental, open to all kinds of people, and willing to give of yourself to someone who doesn't deserve it at all. Being full of grace is an active calling. As the apostle John says, "Dear children, let us not love with words or tongue but with actions and in truth" (1 John 3:18).

We should also be people full of truth. Just as Christ unabashedly proclaimed salvation by faith in him alone, so too should we be willing to speak clearly about what we know to be true. "Always be prepared to give an answer to everyone who asks you to give the reason for the hope that you have," says the apostle Peter (1 Peter 3:15). This is not always easy. It means we need to do our homework and be prepared for an onslaught of tough questions and criticisms. It may mean being ridiculed for holding onto "an outdated and irrelevant faith" or perhaps even being deserted by people we thought were friends. But being full of truth is essential to living out the fullness of the gospel. Jesus never held back the hard truth or couched it in palatable terms.

Being full of truth is also another way of saying that we need to live lives of integrity. We deny what we say we believe when we act in a way that is contradictory to those beliefs. Hypocrisy is despised more than almost anything else in today's world. To bear glory we have to be consistent in word and deed, speech and action. Remember Stephen, our friend who got himself into trouble with Jim Beam in chapter 2? One of his biggest regrets from that whole situation was that he destroyed his opportunity to be a good witness. His final comment bears repeating in this context. "The greatest irony in this whole deal was that the brothers at my fraternity accepted me for who I was in Christ. They hated me for trying to follow them. God is attractive to others." And people can smell hypocrisy a mile away.

Truth and grace need to go together; they aren't set up against each other as rivals. Grace without truth quickly slides into weakness, while truth without grace quickly turns into arrogance. Only when the two come together is there a reflection of the glory of God. If our actions and words are gracious and truthful, we will come to reflect a bit of the glory of God fully displayed in Jesus, the Word become flesh.

Many of us find this way of thinking about evangelism a big relief. Sharing our faith doesn't sound so scary when we understand it is sharing our life and not just a set of rules or steps toward salvation.

The Versatile Evangelist

If you haven't noticed by now, we are big on the value of relationships. Lordship, integrity, and servanthood lead us to relationships through all kinds of different channels. As a means of helping us in our discussion of evangelism, let's return for a minute to the social calendar of Jesus.

If we look at the flow of relationships Christ maintained throughout his public ministry, we find a great example to follow. He could move in many circles, both in crowds and small groups, among prostitutes, tax collectors, simple Galilean fishermen, little children, the leaders of the synagogue, the sick, the disabled, and even the outcast. Jesus had a way about him that made all people feel welcomed and valued. For him there was no separating believers and nonbelievers; he had come to save them all. True, he did have special relationships with the Twelve; he did spend more time with them and invest more deeply in them than in the masses. But *the overall way in which he related to people was lovingly indiscriminant.*

Jesus was who he was regardless of who he was with. He wanted everyone in his life to have a relationship with his Father and so met them wherever they were in that process and carried them along to the next stage. This meant hanging out with the local tax collector and his disciples at the same time, or letting a prostitute adoringly pour expensive perfume on his feet while he was in the middle of a meal. What a challenge this is to us who so often only hang out with people just like ourselves! When we recall, however, that our own sense of identity is in Christ, we are challenged to be more like him. As a result we should be motivated to treat all people as Christ treats us and to love all people, treating them as equals before God, regardless of what assumptions they might make about who we are as Christians. When we begin to develop the mind of Christ in our attitudes toward people, it becomes easier to focus on them and their needs rather than on our own insecurities as evangelists. *The open and integrated lifestyle demonstrated by Jesus gives us a model of confident relational evangelism.*

A mere stone's throw from the Pit and the Pit Preacher's fiery sermons stands a dorm where Eric lived throughout his four years of college. He wasn't stuck in the same dorm year after year due to constraints of campus housing, he *chose* to live there as a ministry. Early in his freshman year he decided that he could serve the Lord by being devoted to that hall in that dorm. He was enthusiastic in his faith and felt strongly that God had placed him there for the purpose of reaching the other guys on his hall with the good news of Christ. He didn't confront his hallmates and make them listen to him explain the gospel message; he lived the gospel message and shared it verbally when he had gained the trust and respect of those around him.

One student who lived on that hall told us about the powerful ministry Eric had there. "He didn't change who he was for anyone. He loved everybody in our dorm and simply allowed the light of God to shine through him. As a result he had a huge impact." We can learn a practical lesson from Eric's example. It is the principle of *taking* the gospel to an unbeliever as opposed to *bringing* the unbeliever to the gospel. If we are living among people, spending time with them and sharing our life, we take Christ into their midst. We don't have to drag them to an evangelistic talk for them to hear about Christ's offer of salvation. If, however, we aren't with non-believers in our daily lives, reaching out to them with the good news of Christ almost always means bringing them into a situation foreign to what they're used to in order for them to hear it. Evangelistic events and crusades are great tools that can work well, but they should never be used on their own as a means of sharing the gospel. Perhaps we could sum up the point by saying that *reaching out is almost always preceded by hanging out and showing an active interest in someone's life.* Sharing the good news almost always takes place in the context of a relationship.

But isn't there a danger here? As with any approach to evangelism, one that focuses on relationships can easily be damaged by complacency on the part of the evangelist. One of the dangers in understanding evangelism as a whole way of life rather than as an activity is that we end up forgetting the need for proclamation by concentrating entirely on demonstration.

Suppose Eric had lived a clearly Christ-centered life in his dorm but never sat down with the guys living around him to share with them about life in Christ. He would have sent only half the message. *We must not forget the central importance of explaining faith in Christ verbally.* When other students see an authentic life that is marked by lordship, integrity, and servanthood, they will soon become curious as to what we are all about. Many of the guys on Eric's hall started the actual conversations about God with Eric because *they* wanted to know what his faith was all about. If they hadn't, however, it would have been up to Eric to take that step. When we feel we've gained the trust of those around us and want to take the initiative in talking about Jesus, there are plenty of easy conversation starters. Ask if they ever wonder about spiritual things or if they have a particular faith in God. I often found that if I asked a friend what they *thought* about God, I'd get a vague and skeptical answer. But if I asked how they *felt* about God, the question suddenly became more personal and meaningful.

The key is to find a comfortable way to *tell* what you are already *showing*. We should remember Paul's proclamation at the beginning of his letter to the Romans. "I am not ashamed of the gospel, because it is the power of God for the salvation of everyone who believes" (Rom. 1:16). Don't be ashamed! If we keep quiet, a lot of people will notice that we live life differently and will respect us for doing so, but they will have no idea why and will stand condemned as a result.

Three Tools

At the University of Miami of Ohio, our sister Susy lived on the same hall as Meredith for two years. They knew each other well and had hung out some in addition to being hallmates. During spring break of her sophomore year Susy went on a Campus Crusade for Christ beach trip where she spent the week sharing her faith with people on the beach. While she was away on break she often found herself praying for Meredith. Although Susy and Meredith had talked about God, Meredith wasn't a Christian, and Susy felt that God wanted her to pray for her. So she did. Challenged by her own prayers and convinced of the need to share more deeply with Meredith, she met her for dinner as soon as they got back. Seeing that Meredith was interested in what Susy had been doing over break, Susy kept on going and shared about Christ just like she'd done with people on the beach the week before. Early the next morning, after a further midnight conversation back at the dorm, Meredith prayed that Christ would be her savior and lord.

Susy's roommate is Julie. Together they make quite a powerful pair! Julie's involvement in a sorority enables her to spend a lot of time hanging out with her sisters. She met Missy for the first time on bid day and immediately took a special liking to her. They hung out and got to know each other a bit, and then Julie, looking for an opportunity to share Christ with her, asked her to join her at a concert where a Christian band was playing. Missy went but had to leave before the gospel presentation. Julie was bummed. The next week she called Missy and met her for lunch. Julie shared about her relationship with God, and Missy was interested but not convinced it was for her. Not one to give in too easily, Julie called again the next week and set another lunch appointment. When they met, Missy soon told Julie that after thinking things through she realized she needed to get right with God. Back in Julie's room after lunch they prayed together, and Missy became a sister in a far more permanent and Christ-centered way.

Just across campus from Susy and Julie lives Jenna, another girl with a powerful story to tell. As a sophomore, Jenna volunteered to lead a hall Bible study in one of the freshman dorms. Freshmen had signed up through dining hall surveys distributed by Jenna's fellowship group during the first week of school. Randomly assigned to a hallway where she didn't know a soul, Jenna got the names of the girls she would be leading and decided to ask two of them, Kim and Lara, to dinner before the study. Never having met these girls, Jenna was understandably surprised when Kim broke down in tears five minutes into the meal and explained how she wanted to know God. Jenna shared the gospel with her. An hour later, back in her room, Kim prayed with Jenna to receive Christ. The Bible study hadn't even begun!

Three different girls, three unique stories, three new members of the body of Christ. What's their secret method? What's the key ingredient to getting someone to become a Christian? Each of them would be quick to tell you that there isn't a key ingredient or secret method—no perfect way to share the gospel. But if we take a closer look, there are important lessons we can learn from their stories that might help us in our own lives as evangelists.

We learn from Susy the importance of *prayer.* James, the brother of Christ, tells us that "the prayer of a righteous man is powerful and effective" (James 5:16). We must not underestimate this power. Susy prayed for Meredith, and in doing so became convinced of the need to share more fully with her about Christ. God not only answers our prayers, he teaches us through them. Praying for our friends also reminds us that it is God who does the work of salvation in their lives and not us. Susy never would have shared her faith with Meredith if she hadn't been praying for her. We need to be disciplined in praying for our non-Christian friends. Bart, a regional director for Young Life, has a simple motto: Pray first. Pray first. Pray first.

We learn from Julie the importance of *persistence*. Julie could have given up after the concert and taken it as a sign from God that Missy wasn't ready to hear the gospel quite yet. She didn't. They lunched together the next week, and though the conversation was good, Missy still didn't react. Perhaps Missy wasn't really ready after all? Nope, Julie knew it would just take time. The next time they had lunch, Missy was the one to initiate talking about God. Julie just sat there and answered questions. She had created opportunities where Missy could ask about God on her own terms and her own timetable. Persistence paid off. In the context of ongoing relationships, we need to be persistent in sharing the truth about Christ with our non-Christian friends.

We learn from Jenna the importance of *preparation*. Jenna didn't have to lead a freshman Bible study for girls she didn't know. She didn't have to ask them out to dinner to get to know them a little bit. But she did. Even at dinner, she could have held back, not wanting to overwhelm Kim with stuff the first time they met. But she didn't hold back. People won't always come to you and say, "Tell me about Jesus," but when they do we better be prepared, and a large part of being prepared is being available. Jenna made herself available to be used. She was willing to meet with girls she didn't know, and she was willing to get involved in their lives in spite of the busyness of her own. We must be available to be used by God and prepared to share the good news at all times.

Susy, Julie, and Jenna all lived integrated lives among their friends. For them, sharing their faith was a constant part of everyday life both in action and in words. As a result of the lordship of Christ in their lives, they desired the salvation of their friends just as he did.

And out of love for their friends, they desired for them to share the same wonderful gift of salvation they all had. Talking to each of them about the different people who have come to faith with them, we were impressed to discover a genuine sense that they felt they had simply been used by God. They were just excited that the Holy Spirit had chosen to reveal himself to their friends while they were around.

Hit and Run or Sit and Chat?

It should be clear by now that the Pit Preacher's approach to evangelism is not the best means of conveying the gospel message. He was heavy-handed with truth, while remaining absolutely silent on grace. He may have had good intentions to courageously proclaim the Good News, but he succeeded only in proclaiming colorful warnings of God's imminent wrath on all sinful college students. Not only did he misrepresent the gospel message, he gave all other Christians on campus a bad name. His was a "hit-and-run" method of evangelism, where he hit people with the gospel, or a piece of the gospel, and then ran out of their lives.

What we are advocating is a "sit and chat" approach to evangelism, where the good news of Christ comes in the form of a conversation that involves not only a sharing of truth but a sharing of lives. In addition to just plain sounding friendlier than "hit-and-run," "sit and chat" actually involves all of who we are, our words and deeds, all of the time. If our motivation for evangelism consists of lordship—a desire to see Christ proclaimed as lord—and servanthood—a desire to bring the gift of salvation to others—then our means of evangelism can be summed up by integrity, an active living out of the life of Christ seen in word and deed. True evangelists are evangelists all the time. If we are integrated Christians, sharing the gospel will be a constant part of who we are. This is a huge responsibility, because when we fail to bring an integrated life alongside God's message of grace and truth, we misrepresent the gospel and leave a fatal gap between our proclamation and our demonstration.

But what about all the different styles of evangelism? Should we all be doing it the same way?

Different people have different ways of sharing their faith. The style each person uses in communicating the gospel will in many ways be a result of his or her personality. If you are outgoing, you may proclaim the good news in a different way than if you tend to be quiet and reserved. Similarly, the tone and personality of your fellowship group will determine its own style of outreach to students on campus. This is natural. God created us as unique individuals, and if we are the fully integrated evangelists we are called to be, we will all have our own way of living out the gospel. The important thing to remember is that all evangelism is twofold. It always involves proclamation and demonstration in a way that is characterized by grace and truth.

When you think about it, God must get entertained by looking at all the various styles of evangelism used by Christians and then figuring out how he's going to *really* make them work. Thankfully, not only does he have a sense of humor, he is also sovereign, and it is his Holy Spirit who comes to convert the hearts of people. *The Holy Spirit is directly involved in evangelism; he is Lord over differing styles and is in charge of the results.* God desires to use us as faithful and prayerful servants in the process of spreading his good news, but ultimately he is the one with the power to save, opening blind eyes to the truth. We may feel it is up to us to convert our friends, when in reality it is God who does the real work.

If we absorb Christ's example of the Word becoming flesh and devote ourselves to a message of grace and truth pointing to the glory of God, there are three characteristics of evangelism we will always hold on to: (1) evangelism is not a special activity but is a constant part of our lives; (2) evangelism involves both proclamation and demonstration, word and deed; and (3) it is the Holy Spirit, not the holy student, who brings people to salvation in Christ. As J. I. Packer summarizes so well in his book *Evangelism and the Sovereignty of God,* God is the one who brings people under the sound of the gospel and to faith in Christ—he uses our evangelistic work as an instrument for this purpose, but the power that saves is primarily in his hands as they work through us.

Questions for Study and Reflection

Study passage: 1 Corinthians 2:1–5

1. How did you come to know Christ personally? What core truths about Christ got you the most excited about knowing him?

2. Reflect on the person in your life who most influenced you in your coming to faith. What was it about them that you would like most to emulate as you share Christ with those around you?

3. In what ways unique to you and your personality can you share your life and faith with the people around you?

4. Do you rely more on your "wise and persuasive words" or God's strength and Spirit to guide your conversations with nonbelievers? What is the role of the Holy Spirit in bringing people to belief?

5. Why are relationships (instead of just words) important to evangelism? Ask God to show you two people whom you can begin to pray for and begin to care for intentionally.

ROOMMATES

The Great Unknown

Corey decided to entrust the identity of his freshman roommate to the wisdom of the housing division and the luck of the draw. It would be safe to say he was mildly anxious about the outcome of these events. He shared these anxieties with his coworkers at the Christian camp where he was working that summer before school started. We'll let one of his coworkers, Scotty, take over the story from here.

"At a staff meeting one night in the middle of the summer, Corey announced with reserved triumph that the housing division had finally written him with the name of his roommate—David B. Spirodopolous. Naturally, Corey wanted to know more, but there was no other information available besides the name. A group of us on the camp staff decided that it was time to take advantage of his curiosity and play a joke on him.

"Two fellow staff workers spent an afternoon drafting a letter to Corey, with the flamboyantly displayed header 'From the Laptop of David B. Spirodopolous.' At the top center of the page was a small photo of a goofy-looking guy with a big grin on his face, which they had picked at random and copied onto the stationery. The letter was addressed to Corey at camp and mailed by an accomplice from another city. It arrived in his cubbyhole one day during lunch.

"Like any person on the brink of college, Corey was anxious to see what his new roommate had to say. The letter was an exuberant greeting to 'my new roomie!' from a very unusual character indeed. In direct and authoritative terms, he assured Corey that there was no need to bring 'an exercise trampoline or a humidifier for the room,' because the Spirodopolouses would be taking care of those. Also, with no explanation, David briefly mentioned that he hoped there would be 'enough space for my prayer mat.' Hmm. Various other peculiar points of introduction confirmed the fact that possibly the most unusual person enrolled in the freshman class had been matched up with nice ol' Corey. It was enough to send him into a panic.

"Eyewitness accounts of Corey's reaction to the letter are mixed. Later that afternoon, when we heard people asking each other, 'What's wrong with Corey?' we realized the prank was a sweet victory. We finally revealed our little scheme, and Corey was, well, more than a little irritated, though somewhat relieved. The real David Spirodopolous turned out to be a perfectly normal guy and a surprisingly nice roommate."

Once you have gotten over the initial excitement of being accepted into college, it is not long before fear sets in. And the fear at the front of everyone's mind is: "I'm going to have a roommate!" That fat envelope you were so excited to open suddenly becomes daunting as soon as you flip over that first page to find innumerable sheets asking you about housing and roommate preferences. You wonder if the luck of the draw is too risky.

The first question many people ask about roommates before they head off to college is "Do I have to have a Christian roommate?" Our answer is a strong yes, no, maybe so. From our own experiences and from the experiences of students we spoke with, we found that there is no absolutely right way of answering this question. Everyone is different and every roommate experience has its unique dynamics. *The important point is to think it over prayerfully and consider how the decision might fit into your goals for lordship, integrity, and servanthood in that first year.* For some, the implicit accountability brought by living with another believer will be crucial to helping keep day-to-day actions in line with Jesus' lordship in life. Others might feel a clear leading by the Lord to take on the "challenge" of living with a student who doesn't know the Lord but who might be reached through servanthood and the day-to-day demonstration of an integrated faith.

Christian Roommates

For many people the decision whether to have a Christian roommate is an easy one—definitely. Having a roommate who shares the same Lord makes life much easier. With the new collegiate world waiting to redefine freshmen lives according to new lifestyles and identities, it is a comforting gift to share the same ultimate goal of living to the glory of God. As Christina shares, this can be a huge help and blessing. "One of the things that has helped me the most in keeping my faith is my Christian roommate. We planned to room together in order to create a support system because we knew our morals would be challenged." We have found that many students share Christina's view. Some planned ahead, others learned the hard way. Roommates are easily the biggest source of stress for students on their way to college. Knowing that you're living with a fellow Christian tends to take a huge amount of weight off one's shoulders.

"But how do I go about finding a Christian roommate?" This question finds its answer in the age-old tradition of *networking* among fellow Christians. Usually it goes something like this: It's spring of high school senior year, and Ben is going off to school at UNLV in the fall. Ben's friend Kate is a junior at UNLV and is very active in Christian fellowship there. Ben calls Kate and says he's looking forward to getting to school but feels he needs to find a Christian roommate. Kate agrees it would be a smart move to make, then immediately begins to scan down a mental list of UNLV friends who might have younger brothers also starting school that fall and also looking for a Christian roommate. Kate makes a quick announcement at the next meeting of her fellowship group to see if anyone there knows of someone else in Ben's boat. Later that night Ben gets a call from Kate. She's found at least two possible roommates and gives Ben their names and phone numbers.

A little networking can go a long way. Granted, it may not always be as easy as calling Kate. If, in fact, there are no Kates to call for help and you have no friends going off to school with you, here are some other networking tips.

1. Contact staff workers from Christian organizations on campus to see if they know of any incoming freshmen also in search of a Christian roommate.
2. Visit the school, and while you're there go to a fellowship group and ask around to see if the students there know of anyone.
3. Put it as a request on your housing form.
4. Visit a local church in the town where your school is and see if they know of anyone.
5. Be creative—there is almost always a way to find a fellow believer to room with.

The important thing is not to get consumed with worries about where the heck you're going to find that perfect Christian roommate. For starters, God is in control, and he already has the right roommate in his plans for you. On many occasions the networking has paid off for people right in time to send in that housing contract. Also, even if you do have to take the luck of the draw and run the risk of living with a non-Christian, it truly is not the end of the world. Eyewitness reports indicate that some students actually had *great* experiences living with and building friendships with non-Christian roommates.

Non-Christian Roommates

For some people the decision *not* to have a Christian roommate is just as easy as the decision *to* have one is for others. Having a roommate who doesn't share the same Lord does sometimes create difficulties you wouldn't have with a Christian roommate. But at the same time it presents countless opportunities. Heather told us, "My first three years in college were with non-Christian 'potluck' roommates, and trust me, there was much of that time that was not easy. But the Lord used each of them to increase my desire to know him and to be able to give an answer for why I believe. They increased my desire to really seek out and ponder how Jesus would respond to them and initiate friendships with them. My relationships with them did much to reveal my own sin as well." Wow. And all that from having non-Christian roommates.

Even some of the worst horror stories can be used for good. During her first year of college, Catherine was paired up with Betty. Early on, Catherine was full of optimism about the year she would have with Betty. Though not a Christian, Betty was friendly enough at first and seemed not to have any problems with the importance of God in Catherine's life. Maybe Betty would even *become* a Christian that year, Catherine hoped. It didn't take long for the optimism to turn to painful frustration. Betty seemed perfectly uninterested in Catherine's faith and values and made no attempt even to show respect for Catherine as a person. It soon became apparent that Betty also had an affinity for guys on the football team and kept a stream of athletes coming through the room for sleepovers. Catherine prayed for perseverance with what was becoming a very difficult and awkward situation.

Meanwhile, things were about to get worse. Betty, it seemed, was a little too willing to help athletes cheat on their academic work. Seeing that Catherine was a good student, Betty decided to steal a term paper from Catherine's computer files and then sold it for fifty dollars to a football player. This was a hopeless situation. Thankfully, things didn't get any worse than that. Catherine endured the rest of the year while praying that God would still somehow improve her relationship with Betty. It was a disappointing time. Three years later, just weeks before graduation, Catherine ran into Betty on campus. Not having seen each other since the turmoil of freshman year, it was difficult to know what to say. Before she could barely get any words out, Betty was chatting away about how great it was to see her and how she had so much to tell her! It was like she was a whole new person. Putting the pain of that first year aside, the two visited for a while and ended up having dinner together at Catherine's house later in the week. As they talked Betty shared about how she was at a point in life where she was trying to dig deep into "spiritual things"—that she was really trying to understand God and learn about what Christianity means. She had not forgotten the example Catherine set for her years before. It may have taken four years, but now Catherine was able to water seeds she didn't even know she had planted in Betty's mind while they lived together.

Clearly not all potluck roommates end up stealing your papers then asking about Christ years later. But as Heather reminds us, the Lord tends to challenge us and impact us along the way. "My heart has continually grown to see these folks come to know the Lord. Having no control over any of this—except to be faithful and obedient where the Lord has me—requires once again that I fall on my knees, trust and believe." *While Catherine's experience shows how the Lord can work over time even with the most difficult of roommate situations, Heather's reflections show that he often provides immediate ways of sharpening us and strengthening our faith right in the midst of it.* It is important, especially for those who don't have a choice about who their roommate will be, not to look on the unknown situation with despair. Having a roommate will be tough, no matter who it is. But having a roommate will also be meaningful regardless of who it is.

Living with a Best Friend?

Another perennial question asked by students heading to college is: Should I live with a good friend from home? Yes, no, maybe so.

Not long after receiving his acceptance letter to college, Sam gave me a call to talk about roommates. A friend of his, Ron, had also gotten in and wanted to be Sam's roommate. Sam was a believer, but Ron wasn't. Sam wanted a Christian roommate but didn't want to ditch Ron from the beginning. Sticky situation for Sam. After thinking and praying about it Sam felt he was being led to forego the chance to live with another Christian and to live instead with his good friend Ron. Less than a year later, still during their first year, Ron became a Christian in large part thanks to Sam's faithfulness as a friend and roommate. Good move, Sam.

The positive side of living with a good friend is that you don't have to deal with all of the stress of living with someone you've never met before. There is a certain amount of comfortable predictability, especially when you know you can expect to receive their support.

There is, however, a negative side to living with a good friend from home. First of all, expectations will be high. You'll expect to get along perfectly well and have a great year together. When this doesn't happen all the time you'll be both surprised and disappointed. At the risk of getting in trouble with the female constituency, it is only right to point out that girls tend to have more trouble with this than guys. Higher expectations led to tougher disappointments for many of the girls we spoke with. Although it does sometimes work out just fine, most girls who are friends from high school don't do well as roommates at college.

If, on the other hand, you and your roommate do get along incredibly well, you then run the danger of forming your own clique of two. Often without thinking about it you grow to trust one another and count on one another to the exclusion of other people in your lives. Suddenly the friendship becomes restrictive. Living with a good friend can be great; just beware of impossibly high expectations and the danger of excluding other friendships.

Making It Count

Everyone's true colors come out in their room. Unfortunately, these usually involve several shades of black and dark gray. No matter how godly you or your roommate are, you will invariably have bad mornings, bad days, even bad weeks. During my first year I lived with one of my best friends from growing up, Jason. We'd known each other since we were six, so there wasn't much left to discover about one another. Our closeness as friends, however, didn't mean we were always good roommates.

Neither Jason nor I are morning people. We tend to be quiet and mildly grouchy for the first hour or two of every day. Eventually, after repeatedly annoying one another, we adopted an unwritten rule that the first couple hours of each day, when we were both in the room, were to be spent in silence. This enabled us to have times with the Lord on our own, basically not paying the other much attention at all. We understood that this was okay and a necessary part of our waking-up process. Often it takes failure first before we find success.

Everyone wants to find a good roommate, but far fewer people are concerned with *being* a good roommate. And yet this is a far more important concern to have. For in order to have a good relationship with a roommate, we have to begin by asking the question, How can I be a good roommate? Here are a few suggestions.

1. Be a servant in the room and work at being thoughtful.
2. Make a point of having fun together outside of the room.
3. Clean up after yourself.
4. Remember to turn off your alarm—don't hit the snooze bar over and over and over!
5. Don't try too hard to be best buds.
6. Be honest about things that bother you. Don't let frustrations build up.
7. Wash your towel regularly—dirty towels smell bad.
8. Ask permission *before* you borrow anything. Return it promptly!
9. Pray for them.

Looking at our three-part foundation helps us dig a little deeper into who we are in our room. Lordship in the room means you're seeking to live under the lordship of Christ and encouraging your roommate in appropriate ways, wherever they are, faith or no faith, to do the same. Integrity in the room means realizing that you are the same person inside and outside the room. It also means that you are living under the lordship of Christ regardless of who your roommate is. It would be easy to compromise on lifestyle issues with a non-Christian roommate there encouraging you along. But integrity says no. Integrity in the room also means having the same high standards in your relationship with your roommate that you have with other people whom you see less often and are easier to get along with as a result. Servanthood in the room is perhaps the most radical concept and therefore can have a great impact on the roommate relationship. Simple things like straightening the room, taking out the trash, and respecting your roommate's space and needs can send a powerful message. Demonstrate the love of Christ; it won't go unnoticed.

One of the most important things to understand is that regardless of who your roommate is, Christian, atheist, Buddhist, best friend, or stranger, you will still face all of the basic issues that arise out of two independent people sharing a small living space over an extended period of time. In other words, there will be friction. Be realistic in expectations and committed to the direction your foundation gives you. The Lord is at work in all things, whether that means spending a year with David Spirodopolous, Betty, or some other student who is just as anxious as you are about having a roommate.

Questions for Study and Reflection

Study passage: Ephesians 4:1–16

1. If you are still in high school, what is your plan for selecting a roommate? How might you network in order to find one?

2. Think of the different challenges and opportunities that go with having a Christian versus a non-Christian roommate.

3. For those in college: how can you reach out and serve others in your room, hall, or dorm? What does it look like to be humble, gentle, and patient in your relationship with your roommate?

4. Brainstorm and write down ten specific ways you can be a thoughtful roommate, including ideas

for things to do *outside* of the room. Keep these in a place where you will see them regularly.

5. Anticipate some potential conflicts you might have with your roommate. What could you do to avert them or resolve them thoughtfully?

DATING

CHAPTER

9

Sarah and I dated for four and a half years before breaking up. When she finally broke up with me, we'd been dating for almost a quarter of our lives. I had been certain we would get married, and in our conversations it had become much more an issue of when as opposed to if. It came as a shock when she finally told me she wasn't in love with me and that the relationship needed to end for good. I was heartbroken. For several years I had been praying that if the relationship was not meant to be forever, that God would end it. He finally did, and I was thoroughly annoyed that he had taken so long in answering my prayer. Why hadn't he ended things earlier if I wasn't supposed to marry her? Why spend so much of my life with the wrong person? Why let me get closer if I was just going to have to pull away in the end? Five years down the road, my heart is healed, but I'm still not sure how to answer all these questions.

Sam and Natalie had known each other for about a year when they discovered how much fun they had together. They started doing things more often, just the two of them, and it eventually became clear that there was romantic interest. They kissed one day by a beautiful lake, and Sam returned home as excited as his roommates had ever seen him. Two weeks later, after a series of misunderstandings and miscommunications, he came home one night angry and hurt. What had been a relationship as far as he was concerned had only been a friendship for her. By the time he made it home that night, the friendship itself was out the window.

Brian and Jen started dating when they were seniors in high school. She was voted class Bible-beater by her classmates, and he class gigolo. She was a strong Christian, and at the time he couldn't have cared less about Jesus. Although dating a non-Christian was not the wisest thing Jen had ever done as a Christian, God chose to redeem the situation. Brian was converted in a powerful way. Now, a few years later and as a newly married couple with a Christ-centered relationship, they are actively involved in ministering to high school students.

Kevin and Stacey were both strong believers. During his first year at college, she was still at home finishing high school. They thought they were in love and had talked about marriage. Over Christmas break, with parents out of town and her house to themselves whenever they wanted it, they lost their virginity together. They knew they'd done something wrong, but since they planned to get married eventually, they found it almost impossible to change their physical relationship once they had given themselves to each other.

All of these people were Christians. All of these stories are true. All of these experiences have a lesson to teach us in one way or another.

Dating, if anything, is dangerous. It can be wonderfully intoxicating one minute, and horribly paralyzing the next. It can be a fun adventure, or a hard slog over rough terrain. Both of us have been through different types of relationships, watched our friends and siblings in them, and talked with others about the whole idea of dating. What comes out of our own reflections and conversations with others is that dating is by no means an ideal institution. It is a landscape covered with minefields, pitfalls, and trapdoors. But when confronted with the challenge to create a better system, everyone is stupefied. For better or for worse, it seems that the institution of dating, as a way in which we come to know the opposite sex and eventually find a future spouse, is here to stay.

If there were a better alternative, say arranged marriages or refusing to date at all and simply marrying a compatible friend, then we would wholeheartedly support it. The problem, however, is that every alternative to dating, every method for having the perfect Christian relationship, every theory on how we should go about meeting our future spouse, is in some way shot through with its own problems. It is impossible to create a method that works for everyone. And so, leaving the doors wide open for many different interpretations on the mechanics of how exactly dating should work, we thought we'd introduce a few basic principles into the equation, in the hope of giving honest guidance down a road that very few are able to travel without at least a few wrong turns.

The Ground Rules

Before we go any farther, we want to acknowledge that it is okay *not* to date. Dating is by no means the end-all and be-all of our relational existence. If you are not dating and have no plans (at least that you know of) to date anytime soon, that's great. Most likely you will save yourself a lot of pain. However, dating is a common reality, and it can indeed be a very good thing, so stick with us as we dig into it here. There is plenty for all of us to learn.

Now, amid all the confusion surrounding dating, we want to convey that the only right outlook is one that has the following qualities: it begins and ends under the lordship of Christ; it is concerned with integrity in all relationships; and it seeks to serve both God and others. These qualities give definition to all areas of life and therefore must direct our dating relationships. Meanwhile, every dating relationship is customized to unique personalities and experiences, complicated by campus dating atmospheres, and confused by different definitions of the word dating itself. Boy, what a mess! But start with the foundational qualities and things begin to get organized. Where do we begin?

First, humans are relational beings—plain and simple, we need relationships. And at some point, most of us will desire the loving partnership of someone of the opposite sex for a lifetime of marriage.

Second, humans are sinful beings—we are prone to sinfulness in all of our relationships. Most students would agree that dating relationships have a way of showing how easily sin creeps into our lives and causes hurt.

Both of these realities, our relational and sinful natures, have to be acknowledged in order to set the ground rules for dating. If I enjoy my relational side without considering my sinful side, I will set myself up for a huge fall. If I am paranoid of my sinful side and as a result ignore my relational call, I'm being equally unrealistic.

Relationships are a crossroads of the vertical and horizontal. A vertical line represents our relationship with God. It is here that we come under his authority and are defined by who we are in him. A horizontal line represents our interaction with people around us in all kinds of relationships. The test of a true believer is to see if the vertical line of lordship intersects the horizontal line of interpersonal relationships. In a godly relationship, horizontal interaction helps to build vertical interaction with God through fellowship, encouragement, and challenge. Likewise, one's vertical relationship with God serves to strengthen and build our human relationships in the horizontal plane. A life like this stands out in sharp relief from the world around it. As one of the most important horizontal relationships in our lives, the need for intersection with God is especially important in our dating relationships. Without question we must bring our romantic lives directly under the supervision of Christ.

It is somewhat frightening to realize that dating is a part of our lives where God wants to be more than just a little bit involved. It cannot be a compartment set far away from the reaches of his lordship. But at the same time, we don't have to look at dating as a matter of "can'ts." Sure, there are limits imposed by Christ's lordship, but to enjoy a relationship along the lines of Christ's plan can be incredibly liberating, given the right attitude. All the confusion, complications, and sin can be set at God's feet to reorder, redeem, and make new.

Because of this need for constant interaction between the vertical and horizontal, we find it impossible even to consider the idea of dating non-Christians. As Paul says in his second letter to the Christians at Corinth, "Do not be yoked together with unbelievers" (2 Cor. 6:14). Although Jen's relationship with Brian (described above) was redeemed in an amazing way, this was a case of God's gracious intervention as opposed to the normal way things work. If we are to date with integrity, the relationship must be rooted in the lordship of Christ, right? Doing this takes two people who are committed to the Lord; otherwise everything is off balance. One Christian cannot carry a relationship. We realize this standard can be the source of a lot of frustration when you think you've found the perfect person to date . . . *if only* they were a Christian. The fact is, God is in control and he wants the best for you. Maybe that person will become a Christian, maybe God is protecting you, or maybe God has someone *better* in store. It's a tough standard, we agree, but if we don't exercise trust in and obedience to Christ *before* we date, we will be even less likely to live it out when we date.

This is all good stuff, of course, but you're probably waiting for a little more practical advice. Well, here goes. What are some concrete ways in which we are able to intersect the vertical and horizontal in our dating relationships? Let's look at three commitments we should all be ready to make whenever we step into a relationship of any kind, specifically a dating relationship.

Honesty

"We seem to be spending a lot of time together—does he think we're dating?"

"We had coffee—was that a date?"

"Okay, what in the world is this girl thinking?"

"He likes to hug me. Does that mean he likes me, or is he just a flirt?"

Relationships without communication are awkward; relationships with miscommunication can be hurtful. If we are going to be committed to godly relationships with the opposite sex, one of the first things we need to commit to is honesty. This is perhaps most clearly seen in the realm of communication. For some inexplicable reason, men and women have a very difficult time communicating clearly with one another, even in everyday conversation. When it comes to romantic relationships, or even the distant possibility that there just might possibly be future potential, the ability to communicate is completely lost.

If we as Christians are committed to allowing God to exercise his lordship over our relationships with the opposite sex, we have to be committed to clear communication. Natalie and Sam thought they understood one another. As it turned out, Sam hadn't really said what he was thinking about the relationship to Natalie—he understandably thought a kiss was a fairly serious sign of commitment. Natalie, on the other hand, was purposely keeping quiet about her intention to enjoy the romance as long as possible without a commitment. When they finally came to the point of having to talk about their relationship, you can imagine that sparks flew as they realized the assumptions the other had mistakenly made. Instead of sitting down and trying to work it out, they both got frustrated and walked away from it, leaving the romance behind, as well as the friendship.

All of us can relate to this story, either through the experience of a friend or through our own mistakes with the opposite sex. What Sam and Natalie should have done is talked long before things could have gotten confused. Sure, it's nice to have a romantic, spontaneous kiss by a lake while the sun is setting behind you and the crickets are chirping. Yes, it does kind of take the romance out of things if you have to talk about it beforehand. But isn't it worth sacrificing a little bit of possible romance in order to clearly communicate your intentions with someone you care about? Sam should have taken the lead here. Guys, it may sound sexist, but you need to be responsible for stating your intentions early on when a friendship begins to turn that corner into a "relationship." Honest beginnings to a relationship, marked by clear communication, are a sign that even if things don't work out in the end, at least the friendship will remain intact.

Just as important as an honest beginning is an honest ending. The simple fact of the matter is that most of our dating relationships will end short of marriage and that a breakup will be necessary. One test of a godly dating relationship is the ability to end it with grace and honesty, and in friendship. So is there a formula for this? Not exactly. You can't always guarantee future friendship, but you can always break up graciously and honestly. These two things go together. It is incredibly important that throughout a relationship you agree to keep open lines of communication with one another about how you're feeling in regard to the relationship in general. There is nothing worse than the situation when one of the two people in a relationship feels like he or she wants to get out but doesn't know how to break it to the other. What often happens is an extended awkward silence, sometimes lasting weeks or months, during which the relationship itself is never discussed. The one who wants to leave begins to feel trapped while the other, who has no idea what is going on, begins to feel insecure. Eventually the breakup comes, and the dumped party is left wondering what in the world went wrong.

A far better way is to share doubts and hesitations about a relationship as they arise. It is okay not to feel sure about things, and it is okay to say so. Agree from the very beginning to be open at all times about the status of the relationship and your level of commitment. If you do this, any breakup that occurs should come naturally, honestly, and as graciously as possible.

Appropriate Intimacy

I knew a freshman couple who began dating each other their first autumn at college. By Christmas they were spending every possible minute together and pouring their hearts into one another. When you're in love, it goes with the territory, right? All their extensive time together was an indication, as I worried, that they were getting *emotionally "naked"* with each other. The following summer they felt led to break things off. It took a full year for them to finally pull apart, and to this day their emotional scars are still taking time to heal.

Sharing our hearts with people we date can be a great and wonderful joy. It is an important part of any deepening friendship to share the core of who you are. But there is a danger here. Although we spend most of our time in youth groups and at Christian camps talking about the need to protect our physical virginity, we almost never talk about the need to protect our *emotional virginity.* Christian dating is not simply marriage without sex; it is a completely different ballgame altogether and one in which certain boundaries need to be set, not just physically but emotionally as well. This is a point we don't often hear. Proverbs 4:23 urges us, "Above all else, guard your heart, for it is the wellspring of life." Our hearts are sacred territory belonging to the Lord. When unguarded, nothing is more vulnerable to pain and misuse.

This may sound like good advice, though you may be thinking, "But how do I go about practically protecting my emotional virginity? How do I know if I'm being too intimate?" Well, we're glad you asked. Here are a few warning signs to show you might be a little too close for comfort. And in the spirit of recognizing all the different ways in which people date and maintain relationships, we leave it up to you to think about what to do if you find you recognize one or more of these warning signs in your own relationship.

1. Your boyfriend or girlfriend knows things about you that no one else knows, not even your best friend.
2. You've said "I love you" without thinking through the full consequences of what that may mean.
3. You spend lots and lots of time together alone and not with other friends.
4. You frequently talk about the future and about the future of your relationship.
5. You talk about marriage and having kids, when realistically these would be very far off.
6. Your other friendships suffer because you're spending too much time with your boyfriend or girlfriend and not enough time with your other friends.
7. In addition to being attracted to one another, there is a feeling that you are dependent on one another.

Keep in mind that emotional intimacy is very closely linked to physical intimacy. When you are close to a person emotionally, physical intimacy is natural and enjoyable. The closer you get emotionally, the closer you are likely to get physically. One of the reasons we stress keeping your clothes on emotionally is that this helps tremendously to keep your clothes on literally! That said, what are some things you can do to keep your emotional clothes on and still have a deep relationship?

1. Spend time together in groups, especially with your other close friends, so you can get to know one another in social situations. This is a great way to see what someone is really like and to see if you're compatible.
2. Avoid talking about the future of your relationship as much as possible (sometimes this will be necessary of course), and never talk about marriage, even generically, until you are ready to talk about it as a serious possibility.
3. When you're together, don't just talk and hang out; do things. Go on hikes, go to museums, discover what each other enjoys doing and experience these things together.
4. Get to know each other's families, spend time with them, and let them get to know your boyfriend or girlfriend.

Before we move on, there is one more pitfall to be aware of. Closely related to emotional intimacy in a relationship is spiritual intimacy. Although it is of utmost importance that a Christian couple share faith and growth together, there is always the possibility of growing too close spiritually. What? The danger here is that the dating relationship gets tied in directly with your relationship with God, to the extent that the latter is dependent on the former. Most of us would naturally think that praying together and doing Bible studies together is good for a Christian dating relationship. Not so fast. It can be good, but not always. Our time alone with God, especially in prayer, is a time of complete vulnerability. When you share this with another person, they become a part of your vulnerability before God. This is a wonderful thing *at the right time*. At the wrong time, however, it can be far too intimate. Sure you can pray together and share your journeys with God together; just be careful you don't mistake the other person for God or allow your relationship with God to become dependent on that person.

Now, having examined your relationship to see if there are any danger signs and having set about seeking to grow deeper in safe ways, keep your emotional clothes on and enjoy building a Christ-centered friendship marked by trust, respect, and contentment in the Lord's purposes.

Of course, any chapter dealing with dating and appropriate levels of intimacy eventually has to deal with the whole question of physical intimacy. The most popular question, of course, is, "How far is too far?" We'll be honest and let you know at this point that we aren't going to answer that question directly. Frankly, we think it's a pretty lame question to start with. If this is the question you're asking, then you're in for trouble. Why? Because the simple way in which the question is phrased reveals a dangerous attitude. When we ask, "How far is too far?" what we're really asking is, "How much can I get away with without getting in trouble with God?"

What we should be asking instead is, "How can I show appropriate physical affection that demonstrates the fact that I care for this person and at the same time glorifies God?" It sounds hopelessly prudish and boring, we know, but if we're serious about glorifying God in our relationships, this is a question we have to ask. This begs a lot of other questions, like "What does it mean to glorify God in a physical relationship?" or "Will the answer be the same for every couple?" We could spend pages talking about the relative divine glorification that comes from hand holding, hugging, back rubs, or a kiss. But we won't. Instead we want to share a simple guideline that has proved helpful for us and for many friends. We don't know where this comes from or who thought of it first, but when a friend first shared it with us, it really helped put things into perspective.

The guidance is this: *in a dating relationship, the focus in the physical relationship should be on showing affection, not on developing passion.* When a physical relationship crosses the line from affection to passion, it has gone too far. The Song of Solomon, in the Old Testament, is a wonderful poem about love, sex, and marriage. One repeated refrain that recurs throughout this short book is "do not arouse or awaken love until it pleases." Although some of the references are less than clear in what they refer to, the overall message is one that conveys the necessity of showing physical restraint in a relationship before marriage. When affection turns to passion, love is aroused and awakened in a way best saved for marriage. Arousing these feelings and creating a passionate physical atmosphere in a relationship is only asking for trouble. And Christians get tempted just as much as anyone else.

Remember Kevin and Stacey from the beginning of the chapter? They were both strong believers, committed to Christ and to purity in their relationship. But after continually cultivating passion in their relationship and pushing the limits farther each time they were together, they finally gave in and gave away the one great physical gift they had to give to their future spouse. This is sad, and worse, theirs is a pretty common story. We hope that it goes without saying that having sex before you're married is wrong. There may be gray areas in a physical relationship, but this is certainly not one of them.

Need a little more guidance on how to have a pure physical relationship? Here are a few tried and tested ideas.

1. Set standards before you start to kiss. In other words, talk about your physical relationship before it happens. Decide what is allowed and what isn't allowed and agree to stick with the rules.
2. If you break the rules, it is important to ask one another's forgiveness, go back to the original agreement, and start over. Whatever you do, don't give in to the temptation to change the rules as you go along.
3. Flee temptation. Don't flirt with it; run from it. Avoid empty apartments, bedrooms, and hiding behind locked doors.
4. Have a curfew. What? Yes, have a curfew. One friend of ours used to describe the hours between midnight and 5:00 A.M. as "the stumbling hours," when temptation is stronger and sin is sweeter. This definitely applies to a dating situation.
5. Be careful about dangerous emotional intimacy. Like we said above, the closer you get to someone emotionally, the easier it is to be intimate with them physically. Protect your emotional virginity, and in doing so protect your physical virginity. This is not impossible.
6. Finally, and perhaps most importantly, be accountable to a friend or two who are willing to ask you how things are going in the relationship and with whom you are willing to be honest and vulnerable. This is such an important point that we want to devote a little more thought to it.

Accountability

The third important commitment we need to make in a dating relationship is a commitment to accountability. At this point let's turn back to chapter 5 and the friendships described there. These inner-circle relationships should exist as a source of encouragement and grounding as we enter dating relationships. Our closest friends need to know what we are thinking and what we are doing so they may pray with us, counsel us, and hold us accountable to standards of integrity. If we allow our dating relationship to distance us from these close friendships, we'll soon see that we have uprooted ourselves and are wilting away on our own. Don't date without accountability. Be sure there is a friend you trust and respect who can ask you the tough questions and to whom you can give honest answers. This applies to both guys and girls. But men, remember you are the leaders of the relationship and therefore bear the ultimate burden of responsibility. Ladies, let the guys know you respect them and appreciate their commitment to high standards of physical purity. Honor one another by not leading each other into sin.

Related to this need for accountability is a deeper understanding that all Christian relationships are part of the wider Christian community. Our dating relationships should be lived out within this context, because they are ultimately meant to help build up the body, not fragment it into cute Christian couples. We should spend time together in fellowship with other believers. This doesn't mean the relationship has to be totally open to all who are interested in the nitty-gritty details, but that there is a genuine sense that you are a part of a community bigger than just the two of you.

Unfortunately, one of the ugliest things about Christian subcultures at college is how rife they can be with gossip. One of the most harmful areas of gossip is dating. We gossip, for example, by sharing "prayer concerns" about others we have no business sharing. If the relationship doesn't involve me, it doesn't involve me. Don't let gossip destroy the trust that should be there among fellow Christians; it only serves to break down community when community should be all about building up.

Dating, as a means of finding the perfect spouse, is not an art form that can be practiced and perfected. Nor is it a game of chance, like winning the lottery. It is, instead, a way in which God can show his power and providence within the human situation. It is an area of our lives that through hope, prayer, discipline, and a commitment to high standards of purity, God decides to show his grace. In talking with married friends, one of the most often repeated ways of describing how they came to be married is that the whole relationship was a wonderful gift from God. Everyone we know who is happily married would say that their marriage has more to do with God's goodness than with how they went about dating. They are quick to point out that their spouse, and the marriage as a whole, is a wonderful, mysterious gift given to them by an incredibly gracious God, in spite of their fallenness and sin.

Questions for Study and Reflection

Study passages: 1 Thessalonians 4:3–7; 1 Corinthians 6:12–20

1. What does God's Word say about physical purity? Decide *now* what your standards are and write them in a letter to yourself.

2. Discuss emotional intimacy. How would you describe a relationship that is going too far? What should cross-gender friendships look like (or *not* look like)?

3. If you are in a serious dating relationship, who are you accountable to? What are five questions you should be asked on a regular basis, and what close friend can you trust to ask them?

4. Whether you are in a dating relationship or not, how can you prepare yourself at this point in time to be a godly spouse? What characteristics do you need to work on as you consider the possibility of sharing your life with someone else?

5. Think of some situations that could be tempting for you or might have the appearance of impropriety for others.

THE FAMILY AT HOME

Failing Ungracefully

I can still quite vividly remember one of the first times I went home from school. I had only been at school a few months and was glad to get home for four or five days, relax, have Mom cook for me, and basically do nothing except a little studying. I skipped Friday classes and drove home early on Thursday afternoon. Expecting Mom to be at the door with a freshly prepared afternoon snack, I was a bit surprised to find a note pinned to the locked front door.

"Welcome home! I'm sorry I'm not here to greet you—had to go out. Will you pick up your sisters from school at 3:00? Thanks. I hope you have your house keys . . ." I didn't. I ended up having to climb in through a window at the back of the house. Not only was there no pre-made afternoon snack, the fridge was empty as well. I barely had time to unload the car before going to pick up my twin sisters. Things were not going according to plan.

The whole rest of the day turned out to be a downright shocking experience as I came to discover that although I was now officially on my own as an autonomous college student,

CHAPTER

10

my parents still considered me to be under their authority. It all came to a head when they asked, in that way parents do when they are really telling you to do something, if I would do the dishes after supper. On my first night home! I had become so used to making my own decisions and being responsible for myself that when I was faced with being under someone else's authority, it was too much to handle. That night, I went to bed at an outrageously early hour for a college student—probably around eleven. I was so tired of my family that I had to get away, and bed seemed the best place to go.

I vowed to myself, as I lay in bed that night, that I would deal with it. I would be back at school in a few days and be free again. Mustering all of my resources of maturity, I knew I could take anything for a few days. Or so I thought.

Friday was another long day of adjustments, but I was beginning to think I might just survive when on Saturday morning I was awakened early. Even worse than being awakened early on a Saturday morning was my mom's reasoning behind it. She wanted me to be sure I knew what my chore was for the day. All vows from Thursday night were shrugged off with departing sleep. I couldn't believe it. Hard-working college student comes home on break for a rest and his mother expects him to do chores!

I wasn't much fun to be with that weekend. I was incredibly selfish and complained enough to make up for the fact that there weren't any small children in the house. It was pretty clear as I packed the car before heading back to school that they weren't too sad to see me go. Nor was I sad to be going. As I drove down the interstate, I began to relax a little bit, think about what had happened, and wonder, "Why hadn't anyone warned me what going home was like after you have been away at school?"

Disillusionment, Respect, and a Servant's Heart

There is an important lesson to be learned from this experience, and it took quite a few trips home over the years for it to take root.

Both Chris and I continued to fail, but at least we knew what to expect when going home.

Although our vision of who we are undergoes a radical readjustment during the first few weeks and months at school, our families still see us as the exact same person who went away (except maybe for a goatee or extra ring in our ear). As far as I was concerned I was my own person, with no one to answer to except myself. But when I got home this all changed, and it took a long time to learn to change with it and honor my parents' authority. College is a great time to learn to be independent and make our own decisions, but we must also remember that we are still a part of a family.

It is important to develop two qualities in the midst of all this: a sense of respect for the family and the heart of a servant. Our freedom as individuals comes with the responsibility of caring for other individuals, and the privilege of doing what we want comes with the challenge to be a servant. As a member of a family, we have responsibilities and an identity, and although the value of these relationships might not always be apparent, they are something we must care for.

Families are the building blocks of communities. If we can't learn to care for our families, we will find it much harder to be part of a larger caring community. This is tough, we know, because it is so much easier to be a part of a clique at school, a Christian organization, or a group of friends than a family. These are all communities of a sort, and we seem to function quite well in them, so why is family so important? It is because the family is where it is toughest. If we don't learn to serve in tough situations, if we don't learn to reconcile differences, if we don't learn to be a witness to those we know best, we will fail later on when school communities draw tighter, grow closer, and get tougher. This won't happen during the first year or probably even the second, but as we spend more time at school, communities grow closer, and become more like families in every way. The family is where we learn to relate. *It is who we are at home and how we act at home that reveal our true selves.*

As I say all this I realize just how difficult it may be for some people to apply these principles. If I had a difficult time at home and my parents are both Christians, still happily married, and genuinely interested in what is best for my life, how much harder will it be for those coming from broken families, or homes where alcoholism or abuse are prevalent? When asking one friend at college how his Christmas break was, his one-word response was "lonely." When pressed for more information he explained that his father had moved out and his mother had moved in with her new boyfriend for most of the break. As an only child he had been left to fend for himself throughout Christmas. Now *that's* hard.

For some people the goal while being at home may be as simple as staying there rather than running off and staying with a friend. For others it may be to split time evenly between divorced parents in such a way that communicates you love and care for both. And for others who come from more stable homes, you will be faced with similar challenges to the ones that we faced and often failed to overcome. It is up to each of us to apply those two principles of service and respect in ways that fit our unique family situations.

Beyond simple selfishness and a desire for independence is a deeper problem at the source of these struggles. *We have all been brought up to believe that we can survive as individuals. We can't.* We need community, and college is a wonderful place to build communities and friendships that will last a lifetime. To insure they do last, we must learn the lessons of servanthood and respect for family at home, as well as at college. If we are faithful in sacrifice and service at home, we will be amazed at just how deep we are able to go in our friendships at school and just how like a family they are when it comes time to graduate.

Home can be a surprisingly tough place to visit when you are away at school. Be prepared. Time and again we would go home resolved to be the model son but spend most of the weekend out with friends because we just couldn't handle it. Most of us have to pass the course on failure at home before we can begin to succeed. But it does begin to work with time, and the depth of your friendships at college will bear testimony to the values of service and respect learned in the process.

Questions for Study and Reflection

Study passages: Hebrews 12:7–14; Galatians 5:22–26

1. What priorities do you think matter most to your parents for your college experience?

2. On a scale of 1 to 10 rate your ability to communicate with your parents. How can you improve your communication with them while you are away at school?

3. In what specific ways does your selfishness come out when you are at home? What are some ways this can be prevented?

4. What are a few creative ways you can intentionally serve your family at home (even while you are away at school)?

PART THREE

realities

"Are you eating healthily?"

I always found this to be one of the more annoying questions my mom would ask over the phone when I called her from school. Did she really think I was going to tell her that all I ate most days was cereal, Dr. Pepper, and cold Pop Tarts?

Most parents are understandably concerned about their child's well-being, and when he's off on his own for the first time, they get doubly concerned because they realize how little control they now have. College is a time during which we begin to take control of parts of our lives previously under our parents' supervision. And no matter how bright the light of freedom shines making college so attractive, it is always somewhat dimmed by the corresponding responsibilities we find thrust upon us once we arrive. Because with freedom comes responsibility. Suddenly, college is about a lot more than having fun, staying out late, and getting a good education on the side. There are decisions to be made, responsibilities to assume, and opportunities to grab hold of; for college is a little taste of *reality*.

"Should I join a fraternity?"

"That band needs a guitarist; I'm up for it!"

"Should I go to that party?"

"Will one sip of beer really matter?"

"If I skip lunch every day, I'll lose weight."

"That class doesn't really matter; I can always get the notes."

"I think I'll sleep in and skip church— I go to fellowship on Wednesdays anyway."

"Should I go out of town for the weekend . . . or study?"

"What should I do this summer?"

"How in the world do I go about opening a bank account?"

"Does it really matter if I don't pay off my credit card this month?"

The reality of decisions to be made, responsibilities to be met, and opportunities to choose between makes freedom and independence seem a little less thrilling after all.

Yep, it's one of those things that comes with having to face up to being on our own and taking responsibility for ourselves. But the good news is that if you're well prepared, organized, and aware of these things ahead of time, the transition to responsible independence can be surprisingly smooth, dare we say . . . fun? From time management to drinking at parties to social activities to financial woes, this next section deals with the day-to-day realities of life on your own.

CHAOS AND CALENDARS

8:00 A.M. Never Seemed So Early

Alexander is a wonderful friend. He is also one of the craziest people I know. His list of collegiate adventures is the stuff great roommate stories are made of. As a freshman Alex had a problem with one of his classes. The problem was that it began at 8:00 A.M. three days a week. Unfortunately, Alex had a bit more difficulty than the average student getting up in the morning. On several occasions while in his room that year, I counted no less than five alarm clocks scattered throughout the room. His strategy was to set them for different times, all a few minutes apart, so as to insure his timely departure from bed. Somehow, contrary to all laws of nature, they failed to do the job. Alex was in trouble. Two-thirds of the way through the semester his professor called him into his office to inform him that if he missed one more class, he would fail for the semester.

Knowing that a sixth alarm clock would make little difference, Alex had to come up with an alternative plan. Out of desperation he latched onto the only thing that would work. Thanks to a strictly enforced honor code, many of the buildings on Alex's campus stay open twenty-four hours a day.

So on Sunday, Tuesday, and Thursday nights, sometime before sleep overtook him, Alex would walk across the street, into the building that housed his 8:00 A.M. class, and curl up for the night at one of the desks. He never missed the class again.

Of course, Alex's story is a bit unusual, but I venture to say he is not alone in his struggle with the clock. All of us in some way can relate to the temptation of the snooze bar, the trouble of getting to class on time, and the annoyance of having to keep to a schedule.

Time Is Ticking Away

One of the great freedoms of college life is that you no longer have Mom or Dad around nagging you to go to bed or get out of bed, to go to school on time or get home in time for dinner. No longer do you have to conform to someone else's schedule. Although you have to go to classes in order to pass them and stay at college, you are, in general, master of your own time. Learning to manage that time is one of the first lessons every college student must learn in order to stay afloat in a sea that can easily capsize life.

Time management. Yuck. No one likes to talk about it, but whether we like it or not, we all manage our time in one way or another. Some do it well; some do it incredibly poorly. For the Christian student, there is no excuse for managing your time poorly; although this may come as a surprise, good time management is a crucial part of living an integrated life under the lordship of Christ.

Good time management is principally an issue of *stewardship*. What is stewardship? The general definition of stewardship is "the act or task of managing the property of another person." A good steward is someone who does this wisely, making the most of what they have been given. Remember the parable of the talents in Matthew 25? A man goes away on a long trip and decides to give several of his servants some money (talents) to manage on his behalf. The master eventually returns from his journey to find that two of the three have invested the money wisely and as a result doubled the amounts they were given. To each of them he says, "Well done, good and faithful servant! You have been faithful with a few things; I will put you in charge of many things. Come and share your master's happiness!" The third servant, however, had buried his money in the ground and earned nothing, not even a little interest at the bank. To him the master says, "You wicked, lazy servant! . . . You should have put my money on deposit with the bankers, so that when I returned I would have received it back with interest. Take the talent from him and give it to the one who has the ten talents. For everyone who has will be given more, and he will have an abundance. Whoever does not have, even what he has will be taken from him."

The servants who had been good stewards were amply rewarded for their wise and faithful work. The lazy steward, on the other hand, was severely punished and cast out of the house. We must be wise stewards of all that God has given us. Everything from our skills and talents, to money, property, and especially time.

We tend to think of time as our own, to do with as we please. We talk about tithing our income to the church or using our gifts for the service of God, but rarely do we talk about using our time wisely. And yet, our lives are the greatest gift we have from God. They mark an investment on God's part, so that our time on earth doesn't belong to us, but to God. Thus, though we may think we are able to do what we wish with our time, we will actually be held accountable to God for how we use it.

Up until college we've been under the direction of different people during different times of the day, from parents to coaches to teachers. They have, more or less, been responsible for making us use our time well. Now that we are on our own we have the opportunity to do this for ourselves.

Calendars and Checklists

Everyone has their own way of organizing their time. Some people are able to keep very full calendars completely organized in their head. Most people can't. What we advocate in this chapter is an approach to managing time and priorities that some might call . . . aggressive. To be fair, it is not the *only* way, and it is not a foolproof system. More laid-back approaches have been known to work; we won't deny that. But it is the principles we are after, and we've found them most readily applied in the methods described below.

The very first thing a college student concerned with good stewardship of his or her time should do is buy a calendar. Now that's not so bad. Whether it sits on your desk or rides around in your back pocket with you, this is the first step toward becoming a responsible steward. Even if you have a good memory, no one is flawless, and the busier you become, the more important it is to write things down.

Once you have a calendar and are using it, there is no better habit to get into than starting each day by looking at your schedule, thinking about what you need to do that day, and praying over it. It doesn't do any good to have a calendar and never consult it.

As the speed of life quickens at college and the calendar begins to fill up, you will need to keep track not only of times and dates but of things that need to be done as well. From assignments that need completing to friends that need calling, life soon fills up with things to do. Having gotten into the habit of using a calendar, the next step toward a well-managed life is to become a list person.

Some list people are better organized than others. An easy and common trap is the tendency to keep lists on so many different scraps of paper that they are soon lost and life begins to go awry. No matter how you choose to keep or mark your lists, it is good to get into the habit of writing things down. It is a pain sometimes, and it always takes an extra minute to do, but it is invariably worth the effort. If we want to be thorough in using our time well, we should be responsible in remembering things that need to be done. The only surefire way to remember is to write them down.

Of course, it's easy to talk about managing a busy schedule when you know all of your activities and responsibilities. But what about when you first arrive at college and are faced with an almost completely free calendar and dozens of fun and interesting alternatives for how to spend that time?

Making Priorities and Setting Goals

We want to introduce you to a friend of ours. Well, he's really an imaginary friend, but he is still very close to our hearts and will help us look at some of these issues of time and life management from a more personal perspective. Meet Tucker.

Tucker graduated from a large suburban high school in June and was ecstatic to move on to college life at a private university in the Midwest. Tucker enjoyed high school but is ready to move up in the world. He always scored well on standardized tests but had a habit of being a bit lazy in the classroom, and thus his grades weren't all that great. Tucker played varsity soccer in high school but is tired of it and wants to try something new. He was involved in student government and wrote for the newspaper off and on when he could get his stories in on time. He's an extrovert who can't help getting involved in more activities than he should.

Tucker's first week at school left him in a daze. Hundreds of new names and faces, a new roommate, a new photo-ID card, three dining halls to choose from, an electronic key card to get into his dorm plus a key to his room, five classes in five different buildings all on opposite sides of campus, six different libraries, and to top it all off, dozens of amazing activities to get involved in should he feel so inclined. Walking among the aisles of tables set up by campus organizations in the middle of the quad those first few days, Tucker found that he was interested in just about everything. What in the world was he going to do? Or better yet, what was he *not* going to do?

As Tucker sat down at his desk that first Sunday afternoon after a full week of adjustments, he emptied the pocket in his backpack where he'd stuffed information about the groups he was interested in. There were seventeen different groups! The rock climbing club, the school newspaper editorial board, the yearbook photography club, Amnesty International, intramural ultimate frisbee, several fraternities, the chess and backgammon club, the drama club, a gospel choir, the fencing club, five different Christian organizations, and SLURP (the Society for Lovers of Unusually Rich Pasta), which sounded like a good alternative to the dining halls. Excited and yet overwhelmed, Tucker needed some help in making decisions.

It is in moments of desperation that genius is born. And this was a desperate moment for Tucker. Sitting there at his desk he realized that to make some decisions, he needed a structure within which to think about the different options he had before him. He needed a means by which to prioritize his time and social calendar to make wise decisions about how to fill it. It was then that he remembered a talk he'd heard earlier that summer at his youth group. It was on priorities.

Scrambling among his collection of notebooks, he found the one he'd used all summer. After a bit of hunting he discovered his notes from the talk on priorities. Unfortunately, his notes were limited. They consisted of some doodling, a marginal note written to a friend, and just a few lines from the talk. The notes on the talk were as follows:

"It's not what you do, so much as *who you are* that is important."

"God first, others second, I'm third."

"Determine your needs, set goals, and develop a plan of action."

"Decisions need reasons, and reasons demand priorities."

"If you decide to do something, commit to it."

"Don't do things just to build a resume."

"Sit down and think things through before you make decisions."

It was that last line scrawled across the bottom of the page that caught Tucker's eye. At least he was doing something right! Well, the notes weren't much to go on, but they were better than nothing. He knew from the line "decisions need reasons, and reasons demand priorities" that before he made any decisions, he had to come up with a list of priorities.

Half an hour later, after considerable thinking, he produced the following list.

Tucker's priorities for freshman year:

1. Grow in my relationship with God.
2. Be a faithful student.
3. Build strong relationships with the people I live with.
4. Get socially involved in the wider university community.
5. Stay in shape physically.

It was pretty basic, he had to admit, but it would work, and Tucker was understandably pleased with himself for thinking things through a bit.

Clearly, the next thing was to decide whether to join SLURP or a fraternity. Or was it? Although he'd come up with his list of priorities, Tucker still didn't feel quite ready to make the transition to decisions. So he looked back at his limited notes from the summer and found the statement "determine your needs, set goals, and develop a plan of action." This sounded like the next logical step; at least he couldn't think of another one. Looking back at his list of priorities he realized that in a way he'd already listed his major needs for the year. It was by no means a comprehensive list, but it covered the major stuff and seemed to be a good foundation to build on. "Set goals" was the next item on the list. Easy enough.

Beginning with his top priority, "Grow in my relationship with God," Tucker went right through the list and set a number of goals under each priority. Here are a few examples.

Need: Grow in my relationship with God.
    Goal 1: Have daily quiet times.
    Goal 2: Get involved with a small group Bible study.
    Goal 3: Find a good fellowship group to be a part of.
    Goal 4: Go to church each week.

Need: Be a faithful student.
    Goal 1: Go to every class each week.
    Goal 2: Turn in all assignments on time.
    Goal 3: Do the assigned reading each week.

Need: Build strong relationships with the people I live with.
    Goal 1: Do something fun with my roommate outside the room once a week.
    Goal 2: Eat one meal a day with some of the guys on my hall.
    Goal 3: Spend time individually with each guy on my hall before the end of the first semester.
    Goal 4: Go by every room at least once a week just to say hi and hang out.

Just like this, the list kept going. By the time he had thought through everything in detail, he was exhausted. It was about this time that his neighbors started yelling and cheering in the room next door. Tucker got up, went next door, and found a group of five guys entranced by the latest, newly released, fully up-to-date football video game. Four hours, three Cokes, and half a pizza later, Tucker reemerged. Ah, college!

Back at his desk the next afternoon, Tucker returned to his lists. Although he wouldn't have admitted to anyone what he was doing, he found himself actually enjoying it. From making priorities to determining needs, he had moved on to setting goals and was now left to put together action plans. Looking back at his goals one by one, he found some that needed more work than others. By nature, some of them didn't need a specific plan of action. For example, in order to go to every class each week, he simply had to go. That one didn't need further elaboration. Others, however, did. Here are some examples from his notebook.

Need: Grow in my relationship with God.

Goal 1: Have daily quiet times.

Action plan: Get up each morning two hours before my first class.

Action plan: Read through the Gospel of Matthew one chapter a day.

Action plan: Keep a prayer journal.

Need: Be a faithful student.

Goal 3: Do the assigned reading each week.

Action plan: Every Sunday night put together a list of reading for the week and decide which day to do it on.

Action plan: Set aside two hours of study time each day for reading, and write it in my calendar.

Need: Build strong relationships with the people I live with.

Goal 4: Go by every room at least once a week just to say hi and hang out.

Action plan: Decide which days I'll visit which rooms.
Action plan: Keep a list in the back of my calendar.

Tucker couldn't believe that two hours had passed when he put his pen down and crossed the room to his brand-new minifridge for a cold Dr. Pepper. All he found was a cardboard container of milk stolen from the dining hall. His roommate must have taken the last D.P. Hmm.

It was while standing there sipping six ounces of whole milk that Tucker realized he still hadn't decided which activities to do. He'd gotten so involved in the business of setting goals and making action plans that he'd completely forgotten the reason he'd started in on the whole process. So back to his pamphlets, brochures, and information sheets; it was decision time. As he reread the info sheets on the rock climbing club and what kind of experience he would need to be a yearbook photographer, the work he'd done over the last two days began to help crystallize his thoughts.

If his top priority was to grow in his faith and one of his goals was to get involved with a Christian organization, then one of the first things he needed to do was to try out the fellowship groups he had heard about. But with so many other goals, he realized right away that he could only be involved in one. He went back and added an action plan to his list.

Need: Grow in my relationship with God.
Goal 3: Find a good fellowship group to be a part of.
Action plan: Visit every fellowship group twice during the first month of school, and then commit to one.

In one swift move Tucker had devised a way of cutting out four of the seventeen activities, and he hadn't even had to think about it beyond consulting his list of needs and goals. This was working after all!

Rock climbing, ultimate frisbee, and the fencing club. All excellent options, each of which would help him with his goal of staying in shape. But to do all three would take time away from his higher priorities. He had to settle on one. Earlier in the day, some of his hallmates had been talking about forming an intramural ultimate team. Hmm. If he joined them, that would take care of his goals of hanging out with his hallmates and of staying in shape. It might even help him get involved in the wider university community. Several birds, one stone. Decision made!

Yearbook, newspaper, Amnesty International? He needed more involvement in the wider university community but wanted a limited time commitment. Tucker also realized, catching a glimpse of the sentence about "God first, others second, I'm third" on his notes from the summer, that he wasn't involved in any kind of service. Amnesty International was looking better and better. With monthly meetings and a lower level of commitment, it seemed the perfect opportunity to serve and get involved with the wider community. It would also mean staying informed about what was going on in the outside world, something he knew he wouldn't do otherwise.

Fraternities, SLURP, chess and backgammon, drama, and the gospel choir. Oh boy. Tucker was starting to realize that his second priority of being a good student might be infringed upon by further social commitments. He would have to be cautious in adding more activities. His roommate was half-Italian, though, and they had talked excitedly about doing SLURP together. Once again, several birds with one stone, a once-a-month commitment, and not much infringement on higher priorities. SLURP it was, and fraternities, chess, backgammon, drama, and the gospel choir found their way into the trash can under his desk. He could always resurrect them another semester.

Deconstructing Tucker

At this point you may be wondering a little about Tucker. Isn't he taking his life a bit too seriously? Shouldn't he relax and not feel like he has to make every major decision during the first two weeks of school?

Yes, of course. Tucker is kind of strange. But he is imaginary after all, and imaginary people tend to do strange things. The point of this story about Tucker is not so much to say that we are all like him but that we all have important decisions to make early on at school, and we can learn from the process he went through. The format Tucker used to make his decisions has time and again proved to be an excellent one for organizing busy lives. And this is extremely important, because *how we begin to organize our lives during first semester freshman year sets a precedent for our whole college career, and beyond.*

Just to review: We should start by creating a list of our top priorities for the semester or year. To turn these into daily realities, we have to move through the process of determining specific needs, setting goals, and creating plans of action—just like Tucker. Some people find it helpful to break their life down into five areas within which to think about needs, goals, and actions. These areas are physical, social, mental, emotional, and spiritual. You can add or subtract areas as you like. These divisions are useful because it is often easier to take one area of your life at a time, as opposed to trying to think about everything at once. Be warned, however; sitting down to think about these things takes some time.

So what does all of this look like at a practical level, day in and day out, once I've put together these lists and "organized" my life?

Say it's Thursday and there is a concert you want to go to that night. The next day you have a retreat for your fellowship group that begins in the evening and lasts until Sunday. On Monday morning you have a paper due. You realize that you can't possibly do all three things. You could go to the concert and head off on the retreat, but you'd never finish your paper in time for Monday morning. You could go to the concert and skip the retreat, then you'd have all weekend to do the paper. Or you could skip the concert, get the paper done, and go on the retreat. Which will you do?

If you haven't thought through your priorities, it will be tempting to take the most fun alternative—in other words, turn the paper in late. If, however, you have thought through your priorities, you will be able to best decide whether to skip the retreat or the concert. Perhaps the concert is one you're going to with some non-Christian friends with whom you really need to spend some time; and anyway, you've just been on another retreat two weeks before. Maybe you should skip the retreat. Perhaps the retreat is one you've been looking forward to for months, while the concert is a spur of the moment, fun night out. Skip the concert. In all decisions, and there are many to be made at college, it is a good steward who first considers her priorities and then makes a decision.

Activities and Identity

Everyone comes to college with a clean slate. No one knows much about your past, what your class rank was, or how well your high school football team did. College is a chance for starting over in new directions. You can try your hand at drama even if you never acted in high school, or play intramural ultimate frisbee even if you never played a varsity sport. It is the test of a wise steward to see how he or she responds to the many avenues of activity available. Looking back at Tucker's notes from the summer talk on priorities, there may be something further to help out in this discussion. One of the points he didn't seem to pay much attention to was *"It's not what you do, so much as who you are that is important."* This bears repeating, and a little explanation.

One of the temptations at college is to go about organizing our activities and social commitments in such a way that we define ourselves by the things we are involved in. Instead of focusing on our identity in Christ, we focus on the image we are projecting to other people as a result of how we spend our time. This, as we know from earlier chapters, is not a good road to travel down.

Even at the outset of my senior year I was still struggling with this temptation. I wanted to do so many things, especially activities that presented an impressive image to other students and professors. There came a point where I had clearly taken on too much and was suffering for it. Meeting with one of my favorite professors in his office one day, I found myself apologizing for not accomplishing as much in his class as I had hoped. Ironically, I was also there to seek his advice on some *more* activities I was considering taking on. Almost like a prophet, he said something to me that I have never forgotten. "Chris, there are a precious few students I've come across who really can do it all and do it all *well*. You're just not one of those students. You need to be realistic and set some boundaries." Ouch! It stung, but it hit home. Later in the year we laughed about how he had severely humbled me, and I reminded him how much I appreciated his caring honesty.

Far too often we are tempted to focus on *setting* as opposed to *character*. We focus on *where* we are and what we are doing as opposed to *who* we are at all times and in all places. Because of our identity in Christ, we have greater freedom in making decisions about how to spend our time—we don't have to worry about cultivating a specific image. If we focus on character before setting, on who we are before what we do, then deciding which activities to get involved in becomes a much easier business. You may even decide you're plenty busy just getting good grades—a very likely scenario if, like Tucker, you wisely put that as a top priority.

Enjoying Our Freedom

Lest we get carried away talking about calendars, checklists, priorities, and goals, we should remember that enjoying our freedom is one of the fundamental rights enjoyed by all college students. This really is the most freedom we will ever have, and it is only right to take advantage of it. There are, however, different ways of enjoying our freedom, some more appropriate than others.

One friend had an especially unusual way of expressing his freedom. Occasionally, not long after midnight, he would strap on his roller blades and go skating around campus on his own. This in and of itself wasn't all that unusual. Perhaps, however, we should mention that he did this completely naked. You can imagine the looks he got from those who caught a glimpse of the streaker on roller blades as they trod home from the library late at night. This friend will, for obvious reasons, remain nameless.

While being a great college story, there is something a bit questionable going on here. In addition to being illegal and dangerous it was also pretty offensive to some of those he passed in the night. Most people thought it was funny, but I'm not sure this is a valid defense. Clearly, this was an inappropriate way of expressing freedom.

One of my favorite ways of relaxing at school was to arrange a midnight round of frisbee golf with a group of friends on a course we had designed weaving through campus. It usually took an hour or two, and it was a great way to unwind after a stressful day. It was a late night, usually followed by something to eat or drink at the deli down the street, but it was always worth it the next day.

No matter how you feel about frisbee golf, I think you can see the differences between the two activities; questions of legality, offensiveness, and danger were fairly more severe in the roller-skating, to say the least.

Both activities, however, are probably not ones someone in their early thirties who is married with one kid, a job, and a mortgage would engage in. Late night exercise followed by food is not the wisest thing to do, but neither is it necessarily harmful. In addition to being responsible stewards of our time, we need to cultivate a spirit of fun and spontaneity in everything we do. Otherwise, we run the real danger of taking ourselves too seriously and becoming dangerously self-focused. It is college, after all; have fun!

The Sabbath

My friend Rob recently graduated from Princeton and, before going to work with a consulting firm in Boston, spent the last year helping entrepreneurs develop small businesses in Mexico City. I guess you could say he is a pretty bright guy.

When we wrote to him asking for insight on this book, especially in the area of time management and organizing your life, he gave us quite a bit of good stuff. Surprisingly, one of the most significant lessons he said he learned while at college was the importance of the Sabbath. He wrote to us not long after graduation, "This spring, with my thesis impending (as well as job interviews, law school applications, and planning for Mexico), was one of the busiest times of my life, but I felt like I shouldn't work on Sundays. For the most part, I was able to keep from working on Sundays all the way through to the end of the year. The result? I finished my thesis four days early and did well. Similarly, during an intense period of paper writing, I was able to finish assignments early and do well. The Lord is faithful when we keep the Sabbath!"

Toward the end of my final year at Virginia I was speaking to a group of fellow believers about four lessons I had learned during college that had been indispensable to me. I think everyone was a bit surprised when I said that one of the most important things for me had been learning how to take a Sabbath rest.

I had always known that spending time alone with God each day was important, and I knew that going to church on Sundays was significant as well. But I don't think I ever really understood what the Sabbath was for other than the day we went to church. Like Rob, it took the better part of my college career before I began to sort it out, but once I did, it proved life-changing.

So what is the Sabbath? What does it mean to keep it? Is it necessarily Sunday? How does it relate to stewardship? All good questions.

In Genesis 2 we read about the very first Sabbath day. "By the seventh day God had finished the work he had been doing; so on the seventh day he rested from all his work. And God blessed the seventh day and made it holy, because on it he rested from all the work of creating that he had done." All of the important points we need to know about keeping the Sabbath can be found in these verses.

First, God blessed the Sabbath. He established that one day out of every seven should be a day of rest. If God needed rest after six straight days of work, don't you think we do too? It is holy because he made it so.

Second, the Sabbath came after six days of *work*. An important point, which we often overlook, is that Sabbath rest came after a full week of hard work. God didn't rest for two days in the middle of creating the universe. Likewise, our rest should come only after our work is done. This will mean careful planning and daily discipline so that each week we get the work done that needs to be done in order to take a day off for rest.

Third, the Sabbath was once in seven days. Although Sunday is rightly considered the Sabbath, it does not necessarily have to be the day on which you rest. When I was at school I often took Friday as my Sabbath. For two full years I didn't have Friday classes, and I typically had several commitments on Sunday afternoon and evening, to the extent that Sunday couldn't be a day of rest. So I began to treat Friday as my Sabbath—relaxing, getting out of town, doing things with friends—anything but schoolwork.

When it comes to talking about time management, good stewardship, and careful planning of our calendars, it is tempting to think that we can get more done and be more active if we equate going to church with having a Sabbath day of rest. Unfortunately, it just doesn't work that way.

One student revealed the key to the Sabbath when he said, "Take time to rest in God. It's not selfish to take time to rest. You can't accomplish much if you have too many things going on, and you can't do anything well unless you've taken time to come before God." We were made with rest built into our physical and mental makeup. If we neglect rest, and fail to keep the Sabbath holy, we not only offend God, we push ourselves repeatedly over the limit. After six days of creating, God took the seventh day and *rested*. In the Ten Commandments he told the Israelites to do the same. Perhaps we should take this as a cue for ourselves.

Looking back over the week from the perspective of a day devoted to rest and worship helps put things into perspective. It serves to remind us that God is in control of the details of our social lives, activities, and calendar. Isn't it refreshing to have a God who cares about the everyday details of our lives?! In the midst of a busy life the best advice of all comes in Psalm 46:10, "Be still, and know that I am God."

Questions for Study and Reflection

Study passages: 2 Thessalonians 1:11–12; 3:13; Genesis 2:2–3

1. What is your current method of keeping track of your schedule and commitments? Is this grounded in an outlook of stewardship?

2. As you prepare for the semester ahead, think about which priorities are most important to you. Why and how does God care about your priorities?

3. Spend some time applying the "needs, goals, action plan" paradigm to these ideas.

4. Why is it important to remember our identity in Christ as we consider what activities to be involved in? How can we tell when we are too busy?

5. What is your current practice in keeping the Sabbath? What might need to change in your life for you to more effectively set aside a day of rest?

MONEY, MONEY, MONEY

Fast-Food Finance

Please type in your four-digit personal pin number. ★★★★
Withdrawal? Yes.
Amount? $30.
Would you like a receipt of this transaction? No.
Please take your card and wait for your money . . .

And with this brief exchange any college student in the world is fully equipped for a fun night out. No hassle, no paperwork, and no strict calculations necessary. It's even easier than a fast-food value meal. Too good to be true? Yep.

However easy it may be to step up to an ATM and drain some dollars out of our bank accounts, sooner or later the source dries up. And when the dryness sets in students start to scramble for another source of income. This is well illustrated by the scene on the main street of one small college town.

In this town, a well-situated block of ATMs draws lines of students every Friday night from a cluster of classroom buildings across the street. Just a few steps from the magic cash dispensers stands an innocent-looking building with a dollar sign next to a Clinical Trials banner framing the entrance. Coincidence? More like convenience. Students explained to us that the building offered anyone between the ages of eighteen and twenty-five a quick way to cash in on medical research. If basic qualifications are met, so the story goes, students can collect a few hundred dollars by offering their bodies up for short-term cold, flu, or numerous other "harmless" medical studies. No real work necessary, just a shot or two in the arm, a checkup the next day, and two days later, *voila,* you can inject a check for fifty dollars right into your bank account. Those who blissfully frequent the ATMS on weekend nights often become Monday-morning regulars with the Clinical Trials technicians. An easy little two-step, but no way to live.

At any given time most college students are one ATM withdrawal or one late credit card payment away from financial chaos. A standard feature of college life for almost all students is dancing along that line, beyond which lies the dreaded statement "Mom, I need more cash." Even if your parents are kind enough to cover the big expenses like tuition and housing, there are plenty of other costs waiting to crush your savings. Take textbooks for example. Countless students fail to realize the cost-inflated nightmare that awaits them at the student bookstore. Classes require materials, and materials cost *a lot*—say between four hundred and six hundred dollars per semester. Even a used Spanish grammar book can come with a fifty-dollar pricetag. Then there are the numerous other ways we spend money without hardly even noticing—clothes, movies, eating out. I had particularly bad luck with library fines. Despite my claims that the university library system was terribly unjust and merciless, I once had to pay a fine of over one hundred dollars for a class-related book. I still can't find it. Mom, I need more cash.

Money Matters

So how do we keep dollar signs from ruining our collegiate lives? Apart from the fear of financial chaos, being broke, or being forced to turn to Mom or Dad for yet more help, keeping track of our limited resources is an important discipline. College is a natural place to develop this discipline.

Financial responsibility is another issue of stewardship. Applying the same principles we discussed in relation to time management, we should acknowledge that every asset we have is from God and should be treated as such. When we do this, financial decisions become spiritual decisions and take on much more significance than we would usually give them. If Christ is lord of our lives, he needs to be lord of our checkbooks too.

In this sense, we really *can't afford* to be careless or selfish with our money. Credit cards, cash, and bank accounts are in our hands, but they belong to the Lord. *First and foremost, this is a wonderful way in which the Lord can protect us.* Included in the Bible's more than 2,300 verses referring to money are many verses that warn of the evil that surrounds money. In our world today one doesn't have to look far to see how easily money and sin go hand in hand. Obviously we can't just rule out having or using money at all. But we can turn to the Lord and seek his ownership and protection. When we begin to think of our bank accounts as having God as a cosignatory, they suddenly become much more significant.

Remembering lordship requires us to pay close attention to our motives in what we do with our money. This is where we acknowledge the unique standards of Christ and *guard ourselves* against sinful stewardship. Saying, "Hey, this really belongs to the Lord," reminds us to ask, "How am I protecting myself against my own selfishness?" Materialism can sneak in and empty our pockets before we're even aware of it. Americans are especially captive to the strange habit of buying things we really don't need. We crave *stuff.* And it usually has to be the *latest* most *up-to-date* stuff. Other folks on campus have it, so why can't we? It is my money, after all; I can do what I want with it. Before you know it you have a brand new nine-hundred-dollar mountain bike, a fifty-dollar haircut, and ten stacks of CDs. Because of a careless and selfish attitude, you've let stuff define you. And you're probably broke. Part of paying close attention to what we do with our money means taking a hard look at our motivations behind spending it. In this sense stewardship looks inward as well as up.

Financial responsibility is also an area that greatly affects our relationships with our parents. More often than not the money we spend at college has come from our parents. Even if we have a job and are making our own spending money, they are usually paying the tuition bill. Sometimes this isn't the case and students bear the whole brunt of the cost of college. But in situations where parents are directly involved in our financial stability, it is important that we honor them in how we manage our money. This will mean consulting them when putting together a budget and being accountable to them for how we spend our money. This is a great way of building bridges with our parents. Money can be an endless source of conflict between students and parents. Why not head this off by being open, honest, and accountable from the very beginning?

Any discussion of finances would be incomplete without touching on the question for the ages: Do I get a job? Some students have the luxury not to; this is a gift to be cherished. For many students, however, it's not even a question; it's a *must.* Scores of students *have* to have jobs because they are paying for their own education or because they need to supplement what their parents are paying. It's a tough reality, and it requires fast action. Other students are lucky to have their tuition paid for, but they have to make their own spending money. Whatever the scenario, life will not be ruined by getting a job. When we say "job," it's important to specify that we mean *part-time* job—something that would entail no more than twenty hours of work a week. Your first job at college is to be a committed full-time student, so anything else will have to be part-time. Now, how do I go about finding the right job?

Here are a few things to consider. First, try to estimate how much money you would like to make through the job. How many dollars per week do you really *need* to be bringing in? Second, examine your class and activity schedule to see when you will be free to work. Remember that you may have to rearrange things to accommodate the job. Third, get moving. The good news is that lots of great part-time jobs seem to emerge in the campus and college-town environment. Ask other students, check around, see what catches your eye.

Within a week or two of starting my freshman year, I realized I needed a part-time job for about fifteen to twenty hours per week. I also realized that my campus dining plan just wasn't going to cut it, and if possible, I should find a job that would enable me to obtain free food—good free food. Many guys in this position were finding jobs waiting tables at sorority houses during large "house meals." They were making an hourly sum over flexible schedules and had access to lots of tasty free food. After making a few calls I learned that the sororities just weren't hiring—I'd missed my chance. A bit dismayed I went for plan B. By this point I had sampled most of the local restaurants within walking distance of campus. I decided I would seek work at the one with the best food (in my opinion). Within days I was hired. I worked part-time there for the entirety of my freshman year and gained fifteen much needed pounds.

On-campus jobs have also proved successful for many students. If you want to have time for studying while you work, try working at a campus library desk. If you want a job that will also enable you to exercise and work out, try working at your campus student recreation center. Or if you like computers and want what experts call the "slackest" job of all, try getting hired as a computer-lab aide. Most campuses have computer labs, and these labs are typically staffed by one student aide whose primary responsibility is to make sure students sign in on the clipboard before using the computers. Think you can handle it? Whatever job you may find, remember that you are ultimately working not for yourself but for the Lord. As those paychecks trickle in make a point of recognizing God's lordship over each dollar and of praying that he will enable you to save, spend, or give it wisely.

Practical Wisdom

So how do we go about being wise stewards of the money we have? Here are five practical tips for keeping track of your finances.

1. *Keep your checkbook balanced.* I will be the first to admit that I balanced my checkbook only twice during college. This was bad. The first step toward responsible money management is knowing how much money you have. This is a no-brainer. This means keeping track of checks you write, withdrawals from ATMS, and use of a debit card, if you have one. The only way

to do this is to carry your checkbook with you everywhere, recording these things as they happen. Good intentions to do it at a later time invariably fail.

2. *Pay off your credit card.* Notice we didn't say "credit cards." Implicit in this statement is a recommendation that you possess only one credit card. There are very few reasons why a college student (much less anyone) should need more than one credit card. Simplify your life; have only one. Credit cards are easy to abuse, and when you abuse them they fight back ruthlessly. Decide before you ever make your first credit purchase that you will never spend more on credit than you have in the bank available to pay it off at the end of the month. Breaking this rule is often the first step toward financial chaos.

3. *Don't go into debt.* This is directly related to paying off credit cards. This is not intended to mean don't take out student loans to pay for college. For many of us this is necessary and the only way by which we can afford our education. But we all may be tempted by other forms of debt—like credit cards. Don't buy things on layaway—"buy now, pay later" is a sure way to pay a lot later. Don't make purchases you can't afford, and don't take out bank loans to make those purchases. One way to be sure to avoid debt is to develop a mindset of *saving.* Make a point to put away a portion of your income in safe savings, as an investment for the future.

4. *Avoid easy money-spenders.* Most college students are smart enough not to buy wide-screen TVs when they don't have the money. Most of us, however, are less discerning when it comes to smaller ticket items. How often do you grab fast food? How many CDs do you buy in a given month? How often do you go to the movies? Five, ten, twenty dollars never seems like much money at the time, but these things add up and before you know it, thirty dollars from the music store, fifteen from the movies, and twenty-five from dinner out show up on your credit card and you can't pay for them. And we haven't even gotten to clothes yet!

5. *Have a budget.* Budget is one of those words that leaves a bad aftertaste. As soon as you mention it, you wish you hadn't. There are few things less exciting, and yet more

important, than coming up with (and sticking to!) a budget. Monthly budgets are the best. Determine how much money you have available to you on a monthly basis. Set aside about 10 percent for your tithe (yes, even poor students should be tithing), set aside fixed costs (rent, bills, etc.), determine how much money you need for food and set it aside (include eating out), fix an amount for leisure or entertainment, and set aside a certain amount for savings (this is especially important). Once you've done these things, a budget is useless if you don't stick to it, so stick with it. It is often helpful to put together a budget with your parents, because they know your financial situation better than anyone else and working on this together builds trust between you. If you can't face that, sit down with an older student whom you trust and who can help out. Budgets often need a second opinion, and wise older counsel is invaluable.

When it's all said and done the students who take finances seriously are the ones who rarely find themselves in the humbling "Mom, I need some more cash . . . again" scenario. By integrating a mindset and practice of stewardship into all our dollar decisions, we can avoid the pitfalls of an ATM lifestyle, not to mention the risks of clinical research.

Summer Spending? Summer Saving?

"You guys are crazy" was the usual comment I, Rob, and Nate received when friends heard about our plans for the following summer. Of course, this is the sort of response to expect when you tell someone you're planning on bicycling across the country. Crazy or not, that was the plan, and for a year and a half we talked, dreamed, and plotted. No one, especially our parents, thought it would happen when we first discussed the idea, but as we developed our plans, the reality of the dream became apparent. We were actually going to do it—bike from the coast of Oregon to the coast of Virginia—just under four thousand miles of sunburn, potholes, flat tires, cheap food, and unlimited adventure.

As it turns out, they actually did do it—in exactly sixty days. I was lucky enough to join them at the midway point and spend a month in the saddle alongside them. It was a month of soreness, enormous meals, camping in unfamiliar places, and acquiring some of the strangest tan lines ever seen. And it was one of the most memorable months of my life. Who says you have to be limited in what you do during the summer?

It usually isn't until your junior year of college that you realize you won't have your summers free once you graduate. It's a depressing realization, but an important one, and one that should come right at the beginning of your college career. Summers are an important part of college life. They should never be just an afterthought, and the way we spend them can make a major impact on our lives, both during college and in the future. Summer is a valuable commodity, so treat it with care!

One of the first things to consider when dreaming about summer during your less-than-invigorating economics lecture in November is your financial situation. How much money do you need to make this summer? It's unfortunate that this has to be an issue, but it almost always is, and we must be responsible in this area. When you begin to think concretely about summer plans, it is good to sit down and set financial goals. How much money do I need to save? How much will I need to live on? What unusual expenses might I have? Once you have answered questions such as these, it is much easier to consider the options. If money isn't holding you back, it is still crucial to be wise in how you spend what you already have. There is no excuse for waste or unnecessary extravagance. For those who need to earn some cash, this doesn't necessarily mean you'll have to get a boring job behind a desk somewhere, or that you'll have to get a sweaty, backbreaking job outdoors. You're in college; this is the time in life to be creative. Whatever your circumstances and whatever your goals, here are three quick rules for how to spend your summer wisely.

First, have fun. Even if you are restricted by the need to earn four thousand dollars over the summer, you can still have fun doing it. If you don't find a job you like, be creative and invent a job. Start a business. Find someone you'd love to work for and convince them that they need your help. You won't always find the perfect job, and you may have to settle for something slightly dull in the end. But don't give up right from the beginning. These are our college years, after all, and we're supposed to be idealistic.

Second, do new things. Chris and I both did different things every summer. From working at a Christian camp, to interning at a church, to painting houses, to cycling cross-country, every summer was filled with new experiences. Of course, you may have a regular high-paying job to return to each summer. But if you don't, make a goal of doing something new each year. This is a time to explore different types of work and a time to learn more about yourself in the process.

Third, be challenged. It is easy to go home and mow lawns or be a lifeguard for ten weeks and earn a bunch of money. This may be necessary, and it may even be challenging, but if you've been doing this every summer since you were fourteen, it is probably time you tried something new. The summer after my first year at college I went off to Missouri and worked as a counselor at a Christian sports camp. I was in charge of nine- to eleven-year-old boys and spent the summer in a state of perpetual exhaustion. I also spent the summer thoroughly energized by all that I was learning through the challenge of trying to be a role model to younger boys. Even now I can look back on that time and see some of the important lessons I learned. If you have the option of doing something new and challenging—go for it. Don't be afraid to do something that will take you out of your comfort zone and force you to grow. Be willing to do something uncomfortable, even daring.

These are just a few guiding principles to take into consideration as you plan for the summer. First and foremost, be wise about money. Then have fun. Try something new. Be challenged. If you incorporate these guidelines into your decision and fuel them with a little creativity, you can't help but have an interesting summer.

What are our top ten suggestions for a great summer, in no particular order?

1. Go on a missions trip.
2. Study abroad.

3. If you're from the city, work in the country. If you're from the country, work in the city.
4. Work at a Christian camp or church.
5. Travel in another part of the world.
6. Do something with a sibling.
7. Do manual labor if you've never done it before. Sweating is good for the soul.
8. Live with a favorite relative and get a job in their city.
9. Get a job where you have to dress up and be responsible. It doesn't hurt to practice; it's only for a summer.
10. Bike across America. Everybody's doing it, no experience necessary!

When it comes to money and all of the different issues that surround it, the best advice is simple: Be careful and be responsible. Remember whose money this ultimately is.

Questions for Study and Reflection

Study passage: Matthew 25:14–28

1. What does lordship have to do with money?

2. Estimate all of your expenses for the current week. How many of these expenditures reflect genuine *needs* in your life, and how many reflect *wants*? What should the balance be between needs and wants, and how can this be kept?

3. Do you have a monthly budget? If not, take some time to work one out, attempting to allow for every conceivable expenditure. Are you tithing?

4. Think about what you'd like to do next summer. How can you be challenged, do something new, and have fun at the same time? What are your financial restrictions?

5. Come up with a list of several different dream summers and begin to think about how you can make one of them a reality.

FAILURE AND FORGIVENESS

Things Fall Apart

Turning and turning in the widening gyre
The falcon cannot hear the falconer;
Things fall apart; the centre cannot hold . . .

These opening lines of a poem written long ago by William Butler Yeats cast a scene of confusion, failure, and crumbling foundations. He may not have written it as a reflection on the college years, but his description is one that easily fits the experience of some in the college world.

Why do friends, parents, and youth group leaders say they'll be praying for you as you head off to college? Why do some people discourage you from even considering a "non-Christian" school? Why do people like us write books about college? The answer is simple: things can fall apart. You can lose yourself in college. The same is true for any season of life, of course, but college has its ways of magnifying the possibility. As we've shown in earlier chapters, it doesn't take much to get us to the point when we suddenly wake up and find ourselves disoriented—cut adrift from the meaningful things that used to hold us together.

At some point every student has gone down the road that begins with a small compromise and ends in a lonely desert of sin and brokenness. Every student. For some it is a small matter that pricks at the surface of life; for others it is a striking blow that sinks into the soul. No matter how much we strive to live an integrated life under the lordship of Christ, chances are there will be points on the journey when we slip into darkness and sin gets ahold of us. Countless students have shared with us about times in college when things fell apart and how they were able to piece things back together. Other students never manage to put the pieces back together.

The principles of lordship, integrity, and servanthood—taken together and consistently applied in day-to-day college life—provide a solid foundation on which the Lord desires to build in our lives. But this foundation does not guarantee a life of *perfection*. As a recent Yale graduate recalled learning, *"being a Christian is not about being perfect but being faithful."* In following Christ we truly are like sheep following a shepherd. We are quick to be foolish, ignorant, and lost on our own. "For *all* have sinned and fall short of the glory of God" (Rom. 3:23).

This chapter acknowledges our habit of falling short and provides some tools to use in rebuilding the foundation when it begins to crack and crumble. Time after time we have learned that when things fall apart, we must cling to the Lord with devotion, determination, and sometimes out of desperation.

Don't Tempt Me . . .

Temptation is quick and easy, and it promises painless pleasure. If you arrive on the campus scene ready to do some good ol' fashioned sinnin', then strap on your WWAED bracelets (What Would Adam and Eve Do?) and choose your fruit. An orchard awaits you. Take, for example, the true story our friend, an Inter-Varsity staff-worker at a Texas university, shared with us. "During his first week at college, one of the students I work with got drunk for the first time, had sex for the first time, and smoked pot for the first time." This was all in the *first week*. Temptation made its promises and sin rushed in to leave its terrible scars. Amazingly, our friend went on to tell us, that same student made a 180-degree turn. "By the end of the year, he had become a Christian and completely changed. His is quite a picture of the first year of college."

Certainly not everyone's first year at college follows such a dramatic course. However, this student's experience brings up some old questions, ones that are thrown at us especially during that first week or two of school: What are our principles? What is off limits? What makes something a sin, and is it a sin for everybody? Each of these questions is a part of the bigger, more important question: To whom do we belong? Are we ready to claim Christ as our lord and fight the good fight?

When looking back on their early college years, many older students acknowledge that they never thought to ask themselves these simple questions. They might have wondered quietly in their minds about the cans and can'ts of college life but never challenged themselves to give these hard questions serious thinking. One student shared with us how he had simply assumed he could ride the fence and live with both a Christian identity and a "worldly" identity. What he failed to see was the all-powerful identity he had in Christ—an identity that could shape who he was, regardless of where he was or who he was with.

Now, to be fair to his situation and others like it, Christian identity is always easier to talk about than to live out. It takes little effort to say "Yeah, we're children of the *light*," but on late nights, on weekend outings, in quiet and private dorm rooms, the *darkness* of sin can sneak in and make it much harder to actually *be* a child of the light.

What are some common areas of temptation? Where are we most likely to fall? While it is impossible to cover every pitfall, it is possible to group many of them into three main areas where temptation finds a foothold. These areas of temptation are our everyday *lifestyle*, our *self-image*, and the overarching *attitude* we have toward life. Below, we take a look at some specific temptations that represent common traps within each category.

Lifestyle—Drinking

Not long ago I spoke with Bob. He's an outgoing, energetic guy who, at the time, was just weeks away from starting his freshman year at the University of Florida. I wanted to know what his thoughts were, what kind of game plan he had for taking his faith to college. "Well, I've grown up with faith and come from a good home life," he began to explain, "and I expect to find a church there at UF. However, I don't have many Christian friends that I know of going there. I expect I'll party; I like to. I like to dance and I like to drink. I know being drunk is dumb, so I'll just be a social drinker. I also love to hit on girls. Sure, I'd love a girl with a Christian background, but she doesn't have to have it to date me. As to fellowship, I know I'll need it and I'll seek it out some. But I'm not really about it too much. I'm good on my own."

While I appreciated his honesty, it was clear Bob was a little confused about his priorities. He was purposefully leaving a lot of room for compromise and was about to be destroyed by his first year of college. By making the wrong decisions or failing to make the right decisions in how we live, we leave our lifestyle vulnerable to temptation and sin.

You may remember Stephen from chapter 2. No sooner had he shown up at college than he flung himself into fraternity rush and set out to grab some beers and become "the man," checking his faith at the door. He built a comfortable wall between his "Christian" life and his "social" life and quickly found himself in a strange new lifestyle with a heap of heartache.

Drinking is one of those standard issues that represents a lifestyle choice. It's certainly not the only issue we confront at college, but it does keep coming up again and again as students reflect on their college journey. Even at Christian colleges, alcohol and the lifestyle it breeds extend an open invitation to unexpecting students. Jeannine recalled her experience at a small Christian college in the Northeast: "I was into really bad stuff in high school and went to a Christian college to break free of it. But drinking was all there was to do there—there was a really big drinking problem." Ted described to us the scene at a small southern military college where "the majority of the social events revolved around beer. I wish I had known just how large a part it would assume so I could have handled it better. I don't drink, but the temptation is really great."

It's clear that students at all kinds of colleges deal with the challenges of drinking. But what's the big deal, anyway? Isn't it still just a personal decision? To really get to the bottom of this issue let's take a closer look at some of the most common excuses Christian students give for drinking:

"I'm only a social drinker; I don't drink to get drunk."

"The Bible only says not to get drunk; it doesn't say not to drink."

"Drinking helps me build friendships with non-Christians because they see I'm normal."

"It's just one small compromise; at least I'm not doing drugs."

"A few drinks help me loosen up and feel more comfortable in non-Christian settings."

Say it's a Thursday night and you've made your way to a local club with some hallmates for a preweekend outing. The place is packed with students and no one's really checking IDs. You even recognize a few faces around the room that you last saw at a fellowship meeting. Blue cups full of cheap beer abound and your mind starts to consider these excuses. Hey, it's college.

Keep in mind that we believe you should have a good time. But as for the excuses, it would be best to think again. First, if you are under twenty-one in the United States, it is against the law to drink. This is a law, and as Christians we are committed to obeying the authority of our government. Even if it's just a few drinks, it's still illegal. The Bible clearly shows that drunkenness is itself ungodly, but illegal drinking without getting drunk is ungodly too. Second, drinking does *not* help you build the friendships you want. It may very well make it more comfortable to fit in with a group you want to get to know, but the cost is not worth it. Alcohol just makes us better at having bad conversations. If you drink to fit in, you are no different than anyone else—you've given up what is unique about yourself, and your identity is swallowed up in the group identity.

You have put your sense of identity in what everyone else is doing as opposed to the one thing that truly sets you apart, Christ.

If the blue cups are still calling your name, just hold on for a second. It may be a casual party, but this is not a casual decision—integrity is on the line. All the above excuses are just that: excuses. They are lame attempts at avoiding the call to integrity. Christ's lordship defines us, and a life of integrity demonstrates that lordship. When we start to feel self-conscious because we stick out, remember how much Christ stuck out and how being different is a part of the call to being Christlike. It's an awesome thing. Even if other Christians are knocking back cupfuls of beer, it doesn't mean that you should. The decision not to drink is not only one based on lordship and integrity, it also involves servanthood. How does underage drinking help or hurt our efforts to serve others? When we talked with Stephen about his experience, perhaps the most profound thing he mentioned to us was that he might never have even taken a drink if he hadn't seen an older but underage Christian fraternity brother drinking beer at a party. A message was sent and permission granted because an older guy was doing it. What we do has an impact. Your decision not to drink may be an enormous encouragement to one of your friends, or even someone you don't know at all.

The bottom line is that as Christians we are called to higher standards, standards set not by man but by a holy and perfect God. First Peter 1:14 warns us not to conform to the desires we had when we lived in ignorance of God. Then Peter reminds us of God's command to us: "Be holy, because I am holy." We serve a holy God who knows us, made us, and wants us to glorify him in *all* that we do.

Now it's time to get yourself a cold Coke. In one simple decision, you can avoid a night of troubles and establish a pattern of integrity. No Christian student has ever reported wonderful improvements in social or spiritual life as the result of a night of drinking. Many, on the other hand, have had a great impact by making the bold decision to be comfortable with who they are in Christ and not give in to the lure of the blue cups.

The decisions we make about alcohol spill over into other decisions concerning social priorities, standards in relationships, and personal character. Now a college senior, Grey recalls having a rough go of it her first year: "It was a tough experience. I was really sucked into college life—living life to its 'fullest.' Sorority rush began as soon as classes started, and off I went. Both sororities and fraternities make drinking very accessible and really encourage it. That hurt me. I thought, 'Well, this must be college.' Now I look at these younger students doing it and just shake my head. Those old ways just aren't appealing anymore."

Image—Our Bodies

Whereas temptations of lifestyle usually involve hands-on decisions about integrity and morality, temptations that affect our *self-image* involve issues of identity. We are tempted to forget our powerful identity in Christ and seek to find or make ourselves elsewhere. Self-centeredness creeps in as we try to take control of who we want to be, and the consequences can be scary.

A March 1999 *USA Today* news story opens with the following observation: "Photos and articles in young women's magazines such as *Seventeen* and *Glamour* help convince many teen girls that they're fat and must diet." The article describes results of a survey of teenage girls, including findings such as: "About seven in ten say magazine pictures influence their ideas of the perfect body shape, and nearly half report wanting to lose weight because of a magazine picture. But only 29 percent are actually overweight." As many girls on college campuses will tell you, this is not fresh news. The media fires a barrage of unrealistic images that shatter self-image among women. Magazines, commercials, music videos, movies . . . a grand assortment of social pressures make the college years especially a time of self-doubt and even desperation. Before they know it some girls find themselves enslaved to an idolatrous pursuit of the perfect body.

I spent an afternoon visiting with two women who shared with me their struggles to overcome eating disorders. One, Chrys, graduated from a large Texas university, while the other, Lauren, has just started school. "In my sorority, eating disorders were rampant," Chrys said. "One of my sisters was bulimic. She could quote you how many fat grams any food item had." Lauren described her own three-year battle with anorexia: "I was in the hospital this year for several months. I felt guilty and thought I was a bad Christian for it. Why can't I just be happy with God's work—my body!?" Together they explained that beauty is often equated with worth and that it's easy to think you must be beautiful to be loveable. This skewed sense of worth leads to insecurity, which turns into a determination to take control and make yourself fit the current standards of beauty. Today beauty is equated with unhealthy thinness, thus the reason behind so many of the disorders we encounter.

When we turn our focus to the biblical understanding of beauty, we get a different picture. The apostle Peter says, "Your beauty should not come from outward adornment. . . . Instead, it should be that of your inner self, the unfading beauty of a gentle and quiet spirit, which is of great worth in God's sight" (1 Peter 3:3–4). This kind of spiritual beauty cannot be obtained by diets or exercises. It is a beauty far deeper and more enduring than the outward beauty we are often so preoccupied by. Again our standards *must* be different, and we must remember that when we despise our bodies, we are despising the temple of the living God (1 Cor. 6:19; 2 Cor. 6:16).

There is no question that American culture makes things difficult for young women. When the world presents an impossible image of beauty, clinging to true identity and security in Christ becomes a monumental challenge. The temptation is to take control of your image and do whatever is necessary to make it fit the cultural ideal. It boils down to saying, "Lord, you made me, but you didn't make me the way I want to be. Thanks anyway; I'm taking over." Even though the pressures are immense, girls especially must guard against these temptations. Having an eating disorder is not a sin in and of itself, but it is usually born out of subtle sins of self-centeredness and the desire to be lord over our own image. Another student, Christy, shared with us some reflections on her struggle with an eating disorder. She explained, "God showed me that the spiritual cause of my eating disorder stemmed from how I was defining myself as a person. I based my identity on my performance in school, my performance in sports (I play varsity tennis), the status of my relationships, and most important at this time in my life, in how little fat was on my body. I felt good about myself when I felt thin and bad about myself when I felt like I had indulged in a fattening food. Because I placed my identity in these externals, I was left feeling very empty. God then miraculously showed me that my identity lies in Christ and not in any of these worldly concerns. For me, not being in touch with my identity in Christ led me to destructive habits of overexercise and undereating."

Though it may begin as a subtle matter of image, an eating disorder can quickly explode into a very threatening health issue. Here are several indicators that can alert you that you or a friend may be developing an eating disorder. If several of these indicators ring true for you, we want to encourage you to immediately take steps to meet with a counselor and see a doctor.

Do you refuse to maintain your normal body weight?

Are you always unhappy with your body image?

Do you have an intense fear of being fat?

Do you exercise frequently without adjusting your diet to compensate?

Are you preoccupied with the nutritional information (such as the amount of fat grams) of everything you eat?

These questions help to give a better sense of how this image-based problem can turn into a very real health risk. Girls who sense they may be trapped within an eating disorder, or perhaps are slipping into a dangerous mindset, should not feel ashamed or guilty. It is crucial to talk honestly about the struggle, to seek the encouragement and accountability of close friends, and to pursue professional help.

Girls have also said that guys need to be aware of how they are involved. "If you notice a girl not eating, don't make fun of her, and try not to make comments on girls' eating habits overall," said one freshman female. "Also, when every guy turns his head at a pretty girl, it just advances our feelings of unworthiness. We automatically think that in order to measure up we have to be thin." Guys need to be sensitive to the power they have in influencing the way girls think of themselves. Even small steps to affirm and encourage girls can help to counteract the temptation to give in to image as a new idol.

Temptation to create the perfect image can also plague guys. My freshman year I noticed that scores of guys were going to work out at our student recreation center. I certainly supported exercise, but this seemed a bit excessive. One friend spent much of the year lifting weights, running, and doing everything he could to make himself bigger and better. I thought he just took exercise seriously, but it turned out there was more to it. We lost touch for a while, and when I saw him the following year he had slimmed down and appeared much more peaceful and happy in his demeanor. I asked him what had changed. "I stopped working out so much and had a change of outlook. I had made it more than it needed to be. When I found myself looking in mirrors all the time to see how big I was getting, I knew things were out of hand." He had made an idol of what he wanted to be, and thankfully, the Lord redirected his focus back to him and away from his self-centeredness.

A hunger for the perfect body also affects guys in another way, one that doesn't seem to affect women as much as men. Jon, a friend of ours at a large Christian school, surprised us when he told us that the single greatest problem among guys in his dorm was the lure of pornography on the internet. After further digging and talking to guys at other schools, it became clear that this is a problem of epidemic proportions. Because of the promises of anonymity, instant gratification, and commitment-free enjoyment, pornography on the internet presents an incredible temptation. We bring this up not so much to present a solution to the problem (which would take a chapter on its own) but to sound a warning to all those who might be tempted. Addiction to pornography grows out of a number of different problems. One of these is a concern for image over substance. Pornography objectifies women and sex and turns people into images as opposed to substantive individuals. It creates false and destructive expectations and completely undermines relations between the sexes. If you think you can handle "just an occasional peek," think again. Little compromises lead to big ones, and the big ones often destroy us.

We are all tempted by a longing to present a great image of ourselves—an image that *we* want to define and create. Many Christian students fall for the trap of trying to create an image of being *perfect Christian students.* Idols are tricky. They always begin with something that really is good—like health, exercise, and beauty—but if we aren't careful they start to rival God for lordship over our lives. When we let a concern for *image* overtake our true *identity* in Christ, we have bought a lie and need to give ourselves back to the Lord.

Attitude—Our Outlook

Temptations that affect our lifestyle or our image are like bolts of lightning in a bad storm. Behind every flash of lightning and clap of thunder is the barometric pressure. It goes up, it goes down, and the scene in the sky follows suit. *Attitude* is like barometric pressure. It is always behind the scenes, directing the surface events of our lives. Even if we don't feel a change in pressure, we see the results. When we discover sin in areas of lifestyle or image, it is almost always symptomatic of a deeper problem we are having with our attitude.

MTV airs a regular show called *The Real World.* Set in different cities around the world, the show acts as a contrived documentary of several college-age guys and girls living together. The angle of the show is that real people, living real lives and experiencing real conflict with one another, make for pretty darn good television. While the show can be somewhat entertaining at times, it always reflects a deliberately grim forecast. The show's organizers seem to purposefully select participants with terrible attitudes. They are thrown into the mix with each other, and the cameras start rolling to catch the steamy arguments and personality conflicts that emerge. Occasionally there's a peacemaker in the group, but in most cases the group is fragmented. *The Real World* ends up looking like a long run-on skit designed to show, intentionally or not, that attitudes are destructive.

In the *really* real world of college, one's attitude dictates what the weather will be like. Either clear blue skies or dark thunderclouds will dominate, depending on our basic outlook on life. Where are we most likely to fall short? What attitudes make the barometric pressure rise and the storms come on? *Common areas of struggle that we all experience at different times are attitudes of pride, complacency, and discouragement.* When asked about some of their regrets from the college experience, older students often cited failures that grew out of these three attitudes. They were fooled by the lies of their own pride, they got lost in a world of complacency, or they were overtaken by the depression of discouragement.

Briefly, let's characterize these three attitudes:

Pride: Pride has a way of convincing us that we can handle temptation, that we can stand up by our own strength and resolve. Or worse, pride talks us into sin through an "I can do what I want" attitude where we throw off the "bondage" of integrity and make our own rules. Because all sin, at root, is an act of placing ourselves ahead of God, the attitude of pride lies behind every sin.

Complacency: Complacency is often characterized by boredom or frustration with the Christian life. We lose sight of our first love in Christ and become numb to all the implications of the faith. Christian fellowship becomes tiresome and redundant to us, and we decide to take a break from all that Christian stuff. Complacency can also lead to overall laziness that pulls us away from our responsibilities and commitments.

Discouragement: While pride grows out of selfishness and false confidence, and complacency out of a lazy heart, discouragement is often spawned by allowing a negative and downcast spirit to get ahold of us. We fix our thoughts on the burdens and hopeless challenges of each day and let disappointments defeat us. Sometimes this is a simple tendency to see the glass half-empty. Other times it comes in the face of a very real letdown—a poor grade, a missed opportunity, some rejection.

Taken on their own or all together, these attitudes apply the pressure behind the weather of each day. The power we let them have over us will determine the harshness of the storm. New believers, old believers, freshmen, seniors—we are all weak. No matter how strong our commitment to the foundation Christ gives us, we are prone to wander away from what we know to be right. Are there ways to rebuild once things have fallen down around us? If there were a perfect formula for avoiding these trapdoors and pitfalls, we'd proclaim it. Of course, no formula guarantees such things. This doesn't mean we go down without a fight, not at all; we take temptation head-on and wrestle it with all we've got. But we are fallen creatures, and we will lose some of these fights. That said, is there any hope?

Putting Things Back Together

Have you ever heard someone give their testimony? A testimony is intended to be a short talk—often before a group—in which a person tells of the work God has done in his or her life. The person giving the testimony will frequently share about a point in life where things had fallen apart and they came to understand the need for walking with the Lord in a more real and complete way. As the talk draws to a close you can tell that through their experience the person has acquired a new kind of reliance on the Lord—that they are working alongside *him* according to *his* plan for putting things back together, one brick at a time. Testimonies teach us about starting over.

It should be clear by now that when things fall apart, it isn't always a mighty collapse. Sometimes we fail in small ways and things only slip apart a bit. But however small, even the little failures add to the momentum that can generate a life-changing collapse. We would all prefer that the lessons of sin and repentance be learned through the small failures so that our foundation is merely fractured and not shattered. When things really do fall apart for students, however, their brokenness is much more vivid, and the lessons we can learn about starting over are easier to see.

Brad started college full of enthusiasm and confidence in his skills as a student. Things didn't go as expected, and a string of poor grades caused him to lose his scholarship and leave his Colorado university. After a while he wrote several of us over e-mail: "Many of you know that I've had a humbling experience involving school. And life really could be worse and I'm thankful it's not. But more important is that every day I wake up with a content and grateful heart for God—for what he has already given me in this life. God taught me a lesson: Never quit. Not ever. I need to trust God every day for the confidence to come back to school and get a degree.

And I have to say, friends, I must trust God every day to complete each of my assignments. My confidence in academics took a hard hit. It's a lot of hours and hard work. I've always gotten good grades in school and never anticipated this kind of thing happening to me. So I ask for you to pray for me to have confidence and make good decisions regarding school. And for the character to stick with it and make the grades I need to go back."

Rebecca's life came crashing down during her first year of school. A blend of image and attitude failures gained a tight grip on her life. She wrote to a group of us: "For those of you who don't know, I took a medical leave from school my second semester due to a depression (something I had been battling for five years but it didn't come to a head until my first semester of college!). . . . I was at the point of not wanting to live; I was unhappy and struggled with eating disorders and all kinds of stuff. I wasn't going to tell anyone about my 'poor ole' depression problem, but each of you is my friend, and all of you are at liberty to know. Fortunately, as each day goes by more and more of the 'old me' is left behind (don't worry, that's good). Now, don't get me wrong; every day is a struggle, but I have the strength now to fight for 'life,' and I mean that literally. . . . I plan on returning to school in the fall."

If Brad and Rebecca were to share about these experiences before a group of college students, it would be a powerful pair of testimonies. The messages would likely hit home with a lot of the students in the room. We all experience failure; this makes us all the more ready to hear about the experiences of how others began to put things back together. We love to hear about healing because we long to experience it. Whether we have failed and been broken in ways similar to Brad and Rebecca or have simply begun to feel things slipping apart in small ways, there are several simple steps we need to commit to in order to get back on track and truly grow from our disappointments.

First, we need to recognize our failure and affirm our absolute need for the Lord. We must admit that we blew it, be honest with ourselves about our failure, and see that our own power will not fix it. This is hard on our pride, but our pride started all the trouble, so it shouldn't have any say at this point.

Second, we need to confess our sin to the Lord and ask for his forgiveness. When pride is out of the way, this is a very natural thing for us to do. It involves getting on our knees (figuratively and even sometimes literally) in prayer and telling the Lord that we are sinful and need to be healed by his forgiving grace.

Third, we need to get out of isolation and into the inner circle. Sin has a way of isolating us—of pulling us off into selfishness and solitude. As discussed in earlier chapters, each of us has an immense need for a small circle of close friends who share a commitment to the foundation of our faith. These are our loving brothers or sisters in Christ, and when sin has broken us, we need to be sure we are not alone. We need to share our failure with them and ask them to walk alongside us as we rebuild.

Fourth, we need the accountability of the inner circle to send us off on the road to repentance. Once we have reaffirmed the crucial role these friendships play, we need to set a standard of using them to help us truly repent and move forward. Repentance from sins is the day-to-day work that comes after confessing sins. If you are walking north on a road of failure and sin, repentance means turning around and walking south on a road of recovery. It is reversing the momentum of sin in our lives—putting commitment behind our confessions. Without the loving accountability and encouragement of close friends, we are doomed to fall again and again.

Finally, we need to cling to Christ as Lord. Giving up our pride not only comes when we confess our sins, it must also become a daily habit. When we emerge from the depths of failure we see that it is Christ, not us, who does the work of rebuilding. We follow him obediently through the midst of it while relying on his healing hand. Only by developing a true reliance on the Lord will we live in a way that reflects our redemption and is sustained daily by his loving faithfulness.

The potential for failure and heartache at college is real indeed. All of us will fail in different ways, some big, some small. The real test of the believer comes not in one's ability to avoid failure, as this is impossible, but in one's ability to recover and rebuild. It takes hard work and daily discipline to live faithful lives. Thankfully, the hard work and discipline are rooted in God's boundless grace, which undergirds our identity in him and strengthens us as we seek to live according to his will.

Questions for Study and Reflection

Study passages: Psalm 51; Psalm 139

1. Reflect on a past struggle in your life. How did God use it to teach you? How did you grow as a result?

2. What is your position on drinking (underage, social, binge)? Is this consistent with God's Word? In what ways is drinking an issue of integrity?

3. How would you describe your self-image? How would you describe God's image of you? How do the two differ, and what can you learn about yourself from what God thinks of you?

4. Are you more prone to failure due to pride, complacency, or discouragement? In what ways can you protect against these potential attitude pitfalls?

5. Is there someone in your life right now who could use your help as they struggle with failure or sin?

PART FOUR

academics

I recently had tea with an older friend at the British Library in London. Mary is in her late twenties and was in England finishing up a Ph.D. She's one of those people I could talk with for hours on end without getting bored.

Naturally, during the course of our several hours over tea, the subject of college life came up. Mary went to a medium-sized private college and is doing her Ph.D. at a large public school. She has a sharp mind and ready wit, and had a lot to say about Christian students' attitudes toward school and studying. Having taught discussion sections for undergrad courses during her time as a grad student, she has a special insight into the way Christian students treat academics. I asked her for advice on this book.

"Whatever you do, John," she said, leaning on the table for emphasis, "don't downplay the importance of academics. Too many Christian students treat studying and classes as if they were at the bottom of their list of priorities." Having been guilty of this myself, I nod-ded in somewhat embarrassed agreement. She went on.

"Make sure you remind them that the primary reason they are at college is to get an education, to grow in the use of their mind, and to learn how to think critically, creatively, and constructively. There is nothing worse than a bright Christian student failing to take her education seriously because she is too interested in other things while at school. It is an abuse of time and money, and a failure to take seriously the gifts God has given you."

I've thought a lot about this conversation since then. Academics is a serious business, and the danger in a book like this, which tries to lay out practical advice for all facets of college life, is to give academics short shrift because it's not the most fun topic to read about. We've left it for last for two reasons. First of all, we knew that no one would read a book that starts out talking about academics. We needed to coax you in first! But second, and more important, in some ways we've saved the most important for last.

THE CHRISTIAN MIND

Now that you've made it to the last section of the book, we feel we can be honest with you. It's hard for us to admit, but we think you need to know that we both believe in aliens. That's right, aliens. And what might be even harder to swallow is the fact that we are both convinced that we ourselves are aliens. Well, aliens of a sort. You see, we aren't extraterrestrials, far from it, but we are aliens nonetheless. *And so are you.* When you go to college with a deep desire to love and serve God, you are going as an alien into a foreign world. Some people may respect your convictions, others may be interested in your lifestyle, but when you claim Christ as lord you demonstrate that you have taken up residency in a kingdom not of this world.

One of the chief ways in which we demonstrate our alien status is how we approach academics and the use of our minds. When was the last time you heard a talk on the Christian *mind?* Can't remember? Well, that may not be your fault. People almost never talk about it.

But some issues demand to be tackled head-on. They have to be reckoned with regardless of what obstacles or attitudes might get in the way. That is the case with the topics in this chapter. As we discuss the Christian mind and explore the terrain of intellectual life at college, we ask you to gather your energy and set your focus. Grab those pens and highlighters; it's time to dig deep.

At first glance, the idea that there is something distinctive about a Christian's mind seems pretty strange. But stop for a minute to consider this idea and it isn't so crazy after all. Jesus said that the greatest commandment is to "love the Lord your God with all your heart and with all your soul and with all your *mind*." We often talk in Christian groups about how to love God more with our hearts, in terms of depth of feeling, and how to love him better with our strength through active service. But rarely do we talk about how to love him with our minds. What in the world might this look like? What is it about loving God with our minds that sets the Christian student apart from every other student at college? How in the world is it that we are aliens?

Truth or Dare

The apostle Paul was constantly getting into trouble. Everywhere he went he would find a way to offend the local authorities, the leaders of the synagogue, or even the local merchants. So it is no surprise to learn in Acts 17 that while visiting the city of Thessalonica, Paul and his companions managed to get an angry mob on their tail. Eventually, their friends had to help them make a midnight escape from town to avoid the trouble.

As a result of their close-call getaway in Thessalonica, Paul and Silas were led to a nearby town called Berea. Now, although Berea only gets a few short verses in the New Testament, and even though it seems like an accident that Paul was ever there in the first place, it is a place worth remembering. It's worth remembering because the Bereans were an unusual group of people. It may not have been a college town, but the Christians in Berea were definitely students. Acts 17:11 says, "Now the Bereans were of more noble character than the Thessalonians, for they received the message with great eagerness and examined the Scriptures every day to see if what Paul said was true."

Yes, it does sound fairly basic, we know, but it is often the simplest things that are the most profound. Why were the Bereans more noble than the Thessalonians? And why do they deserve special mention in Acts? They receive special attention because of the way in which they responded to Paul's teaching. Instead of listening to what Paul had to say and simply accepting it or rejecting it out of hand, the Bereans eagerly listened to him, paid close attention to the details, and then took what they had heard to the Holy Scriptures (the Old Testament, for them) to see how the word of Paul stacked up against the Word of God. Only then did they believe him. The Christians in Berea were definitely cut from a different mold. And even today they set a standard for us as a model of how to exercise lordship in the college classroom.

Can you imagine sitting in lectures every day and then going home in the afternoon and checking up on what your professor said by comparing it to a textbook written by another expert in the field—just to make sure he got it right? Probably not. This would seem like an extraordinary waste of time. But this is similar to what the Bereans did. Paul was a trusted teacher and a godly man—he wasn't likely to be teaching nonsense. Even still, he needed to be checked, and the Bereans wanted to make sure everything he said could stand up to the Old Testament Scriptures. Why so studious? They loved truth and were committed to it. They knew that *truth, and teachings of truth, ultimately belong to God.* The trouble was, there were a lot of teachers in those days. And not every teacher was full of truth. So no matter how loveable and trustworthy Paul was as a teacher, the Bereans weren't content to trust solely in his authority. Their caution and larger commitment led them to turn to *God's Word* for confirmation or denial of what he was preaching. Not surprisingly at all, they discovered the deep truth of what Paul was saying, and many came to believe in Jesus as the Messiah.

So what does this have to do with our approach to academics? A lot, actually. Centuries after Berea, we're still surrounded by teachers who lay claim to truth. The academic world is full of competing truth claims. Every hour of class, every chapter of reading material, and every page of notes contain claims to truth concerning a great assortment of intellectual questions about life. Whether it's in geography, medicine, or philosophy, claims are made about the way things are.

As a part of his lordship, God is the creator and owner of all truth. Picture a grand multipaneled stained glass window full of diverse colors and detailed depictions of people and events, brilliantly lit by the late afternoon sun shining through. But when the sun goes down and the light has faded, there is nothing left to shine through the colors, and our beautiful window looks like nothing more than a big wall of dark glass. There is no way to observe the fullness and detail of the scene on the glass without the light of day. The glass without light is like our knowledge without God's truth. Only when the light of God's truth shines into it can all the contours and details be accurately observed and the full beauty appreciated.

Even though human beings cannot see and know everything, we can know that all truth begins in the mind of God. In this sense, just as the Bereans did centuries ago, *Christians today believe in ultimate truth—truth revealed by God.* Although they may claim otherwise, non-Christians can only believe in ultimately personal truth—truth discovered in their personal experiences or jotted down among class notes in accordance with what the professor is claiming. They have no full or reliable overarching source of insight into reality. There is no acceptable and definite standard against which to hold up knowledge—no Truth to check the truths. They are looking up at a dark stretch of glass and don't even know what they're missing. So they're left to trust their fallible professors and often their own faulty instincts. What does this lead to? In the end the non-Christian student will find truth in her own opinions, preferences, and beliefs. This version of her personal truth might be very nice on the outside but has little depth and no real certainty because it isn't rooted in anything.

You'll remember from chapter 1 that everyone has a lord, whether they admit it or not, and that we all worship some kind of god. In the academic world, life revolves around claims to truth. They may be blatant, but more often they are incredibly subtle. Truth claims imply authority, and authority implies lordship. Without the one true God acting as the lord of academics, one is left worshiping himself, his professors, or some vague mixture of both. Although we view our professors with great respect and we take our own thoughts and instincts seriously, our ultimate source of truth and knowledge is God's Word. Thank goodness.

Making It Count

What makes this attitude toward school so different? Is the Christian mind really so alien in this regard? Yes, it definitely is. In the chaos of a whirlwind of truth claims (including the claim that there is no truth), we have a foundation that refuses to bend or break. With God and his Word, the Christian student comes to school resting in an *ultimate* authority. If you doubt that this is so unusual, take a simple poll of your non-Christian friends and see just how many of them answer yes to the question "Do you believe that there is an ultimate source of truth in this world?" We'd be surprised if more than a few said yes.

The fact that we believe in an ultimate authority doesn't mean every question has an easy or obvious answer. It doesn't mean that the Bible comments in detail about biochemistry and multivariable calculus. But it does mean that God cares about every question and every detail of every subject we might study. It means that truth is sacred and that God wants to walk alongside us as we bring eager minds into the classroom. Because God is sovereign and because we want him to be a part of every area of our lives, we must be willing to submit our academic interests to his care. We do this by seeking to bring every class, all assigned reading, and every conversation into a coherent whole rooted in the Lord's ownership of truth and lordship of our minds.

Standing before the panels of colorful stained glass, we have a lot to take in. If we stare at only one portion of the glass, we miss out on the whole picture. Each little detail should be given attention, but the image is at its fullest when it can finally be taken in all at once. This is what we work toward. We give the details their due, but then we step back and let the light spill through all the colors in a grand and sweeping image. When the light shines equally through the panels and from our vantage point everything is integrated, that is when the marvelous message of the glass comes together.

As Christian students and Christian thinkers, we seek to build a consistent understanding of the world on the foundation of the lordship of Christ. As a result we cannot allow internal contradictions in our thinking. The image in the stained glass window can't be one thing today and another tomorrow. It can't be one thing for me and another thing entirely for you. In other words, we find it impossible to believe that something could be true for one person and not true for another. If God's truth is true for everyone, this kind of relativism is impossible. Truth must be consistent. The Christian mind, therefore, must set out to pursue truth consistently. If learning means just taking notes and spitting back answers, a redefinition is long overdue.

When it comes to day-to-day life in the classroom, how do we integrate this understanding of lordship? *First of all, we need to be like the Bereans when it comes to how we treat everything we learn in class.* We need to be active students. We need to listen well and test what we hear against what the Scriptures might have to say on the matter at hand. We need to bring the mind of God to the claims of the classroom. Do the theories we learn for interpreting classical literature in a freshman English class hold up in light of what the Bible says our attitude should be toward the written word? In what ways do biological theories of evolution fit into the Genesis creation narrative? Do our professors' attitudes toward the supernatural fit in with a biblical understanding of miracles? Every class is going to be stuffed full of truth claims. Sometimes they're blatant, sometimes they're subtle. Whatever the case, everything we learn should be passed through a filter that enables us to see it in the light of God's truth as revealed in the Bible. It's a matter of learning to think critically in the light of God's truth.

On another level, we should also test what our professors teach us against what other experts in the field are teaching. Our high regard for truth means we check it and double-check it in the ways that seem wisest. Should we listen to our professors and respect their interpretation of things? Yes, absolutely. But we should never treat them as if they speak with ultimate authority. Just because my sociology professor knows more than I do about American culture doesn't mean she's always right. My religious history professor may be very informed about the early Christian church, but his opinions of it could still be wrong. Professors are fallible too! We should always be willing to investigate what they say in order to broaden our own understanding and command of the material at hand. Hopefully this won't always mean checking every word of every lecture with outside material, but it may often mean a little extra investigative work. Don't worry; it's worth it.

Do you remember Lane from chapter 2? She kept an academic journal throughout her college career. After every class attended, every book read, and every discussion participated in, Lane would spend some time reflecting on what she was learning and what her faith had to say about it. What a model for integrity!

Of a Mind to Serve

Servanthood? At this point it may seem like we are trying to force everything we talk about into the three-part foundation! But given half a minute of thought, it is easy to see how even the principle of servanthood naturally relates to the life of the mind, setting us apart from other students.

Why do most people go to college? Quite a few go to avoid the real world for four more years. A lot go to college to prepare them for graduate school. Some go to get a good degree that will enable them to get a high-paying job and make a lot of money. Some go with the hope of meeting their spouse. And still others go because they can't think of anything better to do and they've heard that college is at least fun.

But why do Christians go to college? Of course, there are a variety of answers to this question, and different people have different emphases. Ultimately, however, the reason we go to college is so that we might be better equipped as God's stewards to serve him faithfully with the gifts he has given us. We go to college to grow in our knowledge and ability to serve him. College is not just a fun place to do a little work and hang out with friends. If we take our education seriously, we realize that college is a jumping-off point for greater service to God through the growth and use of our minds.

Many people, Christian and non-Christian alike, go to college with a great deal of ambition. What should set Christians apart is the object of our ambition. If you have no lord other than yourself, your ambition will most likely be to make a lot of money one day or be the best in your field. These desires are not necessarily wrong, but they are often misdirected. We should desire to be the best that we can be, but this desire is not one directed toward selfish ends. Our desire to be the best we can be should be directed outward in service of Christ and his world. This is a radical difference between the Christian and the non-Christian student.

Of course, there are some students who have no faith in Christ but who still desire to serve other people through their education. These are often very solid, well-intentioned people who have big dreams of changing the world but ultimately very little reason to do so. Some will go on to do great things, while many will gradually become embittered by the world and give up on their quest for utopia. Though they lack the right foundation, the initial efforts of such students should challenge us. It is the Christian student who is called to stick with it, to learn in order to serve, and to use her education as a means of building up knowledge, wisdom, and practical skills so she might serve God and his kingdom more faithfully.

Creeping Anti-intellectualism

During the spring of 1998 an interesting series of editorial columns appeared in the *Daily Tar Heel,* the University of North Carolina's student newspaper. Andy, a graduate student, wrote a number of columns under the title *Beware of Putting Too Much Faith in Your Faith.* The articles were an investigation of sorts into why he was no longer a Christian and didn't subscribe to any set of beliefs. He said in the first article, "I have Christian friends and family members, and I respect all of them. In fact, I myself was a believing, practicing Christian during my last two years of high school and first year of college." He went on to explain how he had come to question his faith and why he no longer believed. These articles generated a lot of responses, especially from among the large Christian community on campus. One of the many letters printed in the paper that spring was from a Christian who told Andy, in an attempt to explain the faith to him, that "God did not intend for us to understand everything. . . . Christianity is not a matter of head knowledge, but of heart knowledge."

At first glance, this comment seems to be pretty good. It's true God did not intend for us to understand absolutely everything about him or about ourselves. But does this necessarily mean that our faith is only a matter of heart knowledge and not head knowledge? On further examination this brief quotation reveals a subtle anti-intellectualism that has crept into our understanding of Christianity and done a lot to destroy the foundation of our faith. For although faith is certainly a matter of the heart, it is also very much a matter of the head. Our faith in Christ as savior and lord is not the result of a disconnection between our brain and our beliefs. God does not bypass our mind when he convinces our hearts to come to faith. No, instead he uses our minds as well as our hearts to draw us to him. True, one can never come to faith simply by proving to himself the existence of God. God must call each one of us and reveal himself to us in order for us to have faith. This does not mean, however, that he does this completely apart from our minds. God works on our hearts and minds as he draws us to himself. Our minds are very important to God and must be submitted to his lordship.

We cannot emphasize enough the importance of one's education and the significance of realizing that the Christian mind is radically different from the secular mind. The best place to see this is probably in Romans—Paul's long letter to the Christians in Rome. Chapter 12 marks the beginning of a section that deals with practical advice for daily life. Paul starts off in verses 1 and 2 by saying, "Therefore, I urge you, brothers, in view of God's mercy, to offer your bodies as living sacrifices, holy and pleasing to God—this is your spiritual act of worship. Do not conform any longer to the pattern of this world, but *be transformed by the renewing of your mind.* Then you will be able to test and approve what God's will is—his good, pleasing and perfect will."

Where does daily worship and godly living begin? With the renewal of the mind. Worship doesn't begin with an outward act, a song of praise, or a special prayer. True worship that is glorifying to God begins with an act of the mind. God must take our minds and transform them according to his Word in order for our worship, our lives, to be pleasing to him. When are we able to do God's will as he desires? When we have allowed our minds to be transformed and conformed to his likeness. We must submit to Christ's lordship and the authority of his Word. We must seek to bring our thoughts into a coherent whole, not allowing for inconsistency or "personal truths" to enter into the equation. And we must see all knowledge, all growth of our intellect, as a means for serving God more completely with our whole selves. For our minds belong to God, and he desires to use them mightily to do his work.

"But hold on just one second," you might say. "Are you saying that all Christians need to be intellectuals in order to be good Christians? What about the student going to college on a hockey scholarship with hopes of nothing but making a great NHL player? What about the future beautician?! (Not that hockey players and beauticians don't think.) Don't we all have different gifts and abilities, with only some of us called to be 'intellectuals'?"

Good point; thanks for bringing that up. It's important to clarify that we aren't saying all Christian students are the same and that all of us should be on the leading edge of intellectual cultural revitalization. What we are saying is that each one of us needs to take the life of the mind seriously. We need to surrender our every thought, our every classroom question, every bit of information we process to the lordship of Christ. Regardless of one's future profession or goals in life, we are each called to a renewal of our minds. Frankly, we aren't interested in creating a bunch of Christian intellectuals. What is far more important is that we all engage our minds in the active pursuit of a faithful life, using what God has given us to his greater glory.

Questions for Study and Reflection

Study passages: Colossians 2:6–12; 3:1–3

1. What is it exactly that should be different about the Christian's mind when compared to the nonbeliever's mind?

2. How is developing a Christian mind an issue of stewardship?

3. Are there any ways in which your faith is anti-intellectual? Are Christians on your campus perceived to be this way? What personal impact can you have to steer things in a deeper direction?

4. Think about one class you are taking. How can you be a Berean in this class?

5. Discuss the difference between being a Christian intellectual and having a Christian mind.

DECISIONS AND DILEMMAS

We've all heard that old adage: "A mind is a terrible thing to waste." It's a bumper sticker ideal that high school teachers love to tell students when the rigors of chemistry class have become, shall we say, less than entertaining. "How could you possibly not want to memorize the Periodic Table of Elements? Don't you know that the mind is a terrible thing to waste!?" Thankfully, college offers more exciting ways to avoid wasting our minds. And more important, having a Christian mind gives us a lot more inspiration than a tired old adage. In the last chapter we called for students to engage their minds, like the Bereans, actively pursuing God's truth and studying for his glory. In this chapter we want to take a look at how this calling is played out in the decisions and dilemmas of everyday academic life.

I Have to Go to Class?

Jen graduated from a small Christian high school in Georgia where she was valedictorian of her class. She always wanted to be a lawyer and knew college was an important step on that path. Though fully qualified to launch into a large university, Jen spent two years after high school at a local community college sharpening her academic discipline and preparing for the road ahead.

Pete is from North Dakota and attends a small Christian college in Minnesota. The summer before heading off to school, he realized he could easily get overcommitted pursuing different priorities. He thought through his goals and decided he wanted to be an "academic Christian" while also having a great first season on the school's football team.

Holly arrived at a private Christian college in the Northeast expecting to enter a rigorous academic environment. She was surprised to find that, for the students at least, college was really much more about social life than about studying.

From very different backgrounds and at very different colleges, these three students share an important goal: the pursuit of academic excellence. *That is, they expect to be the kind of students that work at being students.* And the amazing thing is, all three are very normal, well-rounded, and exciting individuals! What is surprising is how easy it is for most students, even those committed to academic excellence, to spend their time gobbling up the side dishes that college life offers while forgetting that academics are really the main course.

It can be an ugly awakening when you find yourself greeting your first morning at college with the realization, "Oh yeah, I have to go to class!" We want to do all we can to spare you the pain of realizing this when it's too late. As one honest freshman shared with us, "I wish someone had told me that college was work! As a high school senior, you hear a lot about how fun and exciting college is with activities, new freedoms, etc. I agree that college is much better than high school, but it is also more difficult." We haven't found any students who would disagree with that statement. College *is* work. It takes effort, discipline, and sacrifice. Meeting academic goals may mean a few late nights or early mornings from time to time. But good things tend to take work, don't they? They do because they're worth it.

Becoming the kind of student that works at being a student starts with having the right outlook. For Jen, Pete, and Holly, being a student was more than just sliding into the next set of tasks—it was a much greater matter of living out their calling as Christian students in the classroom.

Full-time Framework

By now it's clear that there is more to college than just earning class credits. All kinds of activities, relationships, and priorities blend together to make up the fullness of the college experience. Bearing this in mind, however, we can't place enough importance on the fact that while at school you are called to be a student. If being at college is your *vocation* for these years, being a student is your *occupation*. It's the main dish. And like everything from relationships to finances, the defining component of academic life is that it is an area where we must be active stewards of our calling. We take the tasks of the classroom as a very real assignment—a place where the Lord has put us so we might grow in new ways and honor him. If the goal for academics is merely getting by, then we are accepting a narrow perspective that misses the point. Thriving as a student, on the other hand, means taking deliberate steps to invest talents and energy into the challenges that classrooms hold.

So how do we take this stewardship seriously? What does it look like to be devoted to my occupation as a student? The students who model this concept of academic stewardship gave us a simple answer: *treat your academic life as a full-time job.* If the temptation is to approach classes and studying as a kind of part-time, "I'll get around to it" priority, then go ahead and set things straight by giving yourself a promotion. Make yourself the CEO of your academic life. God is the ultimate boss, mind you, but you're a full-timer and need to manage all the operations with smart strategies and sound priorities. Adopt the nine-to-five schedule and pour your efforts into seeing it through. You can even throw in vacation days, sick leave, and lunch hours—just so long as the work gets done.

The first thing a full-time framework does is set boundaries. It establishes the parameters of your working schedule while saving evenings, nights, and early mornings for other facets of your student life. You have a floating office that moves with you through the day, but when the day's work is done, it's done.

The second thing a full-time framework does is encourage discipline. If you have an open window between your 1 P.M. and 4 P.M. classes on Tuesdays and Thursdays, devote that time to doing the work of those classes. Instead of taking a nap or getting distracted by things that might pop up during that window, make a point of knocking out some of the reading or getting started on a paper.

As CEO of your student life you also have two additional freedoms. First, for the most part you determine your class schedule. Most college schedules offer classes on a Tuesday-Thursday track and a Monday-Wednesday-Friday track. The Tuesday-Thursday courses usually run longer, but you have the benefit of only two chunks of class a week. We'll get to the ins and outs of setting up a schedule later in the chapter—for now the point is to see that you have an enormous amount of say in the design of your daily routine. The trick is to be strategic in setting things up to be a good fit with your habits and preferences.

The second freedom has to do with where you do your studying. This may seem like a small decision, but it is not to be overlooked. *Where* you study will have a big impact on *how* you study. It's going to be an office of sorts, so you may as well find something that's user-friendly. Most campuses have beautiful study spots tucked away in libraries. My junior year I had to face the realization that two years without the benefits of a full-time framework had hurt me. As a small step toward progress, I discovered an amazing part of one of our libraries that was devoted to housing a collection of rare books. What made it amazing was that it was a beautiful place to study—inspiring even. My regular class readings suddenly felt more significant simply by doing them in a beautiful environment. A friend of mine studied in an empty Sunday school room in a nearby church. The building was open all day and she was given permission to use the room. She would stop by the sanctuary first to pray over her academic life, then head to her spot to get to work. Talk about integration!

Bringing a full-time outlook and organization to academic life turns stewardship into a tangible day-to-day reality. It may seem like a lot to take on, but it will save the frustrations of stress and regret in the long run. Most of us learn the value of this framework after seeing how frustrating things can get without it. As one senior who truly modeled her advice put it, "Get eight hours of sleep a night, do all your homework, do the work of a student nine to five, and you will most likely get straight As." Hey, not a bad deal.

194

Professors, Courses, and Classy Decisions

When it comes to academic life, we realize every college has its unique characteristics. Some schools have a reputation for being rigorous and demanding; others are known for their, well, parties. Whatever the case may be, a few things remain standard across the board. First, every college has professors and classes, and a lot of options for both. Second, and not exactly a big surprise, every school has confused students trying to wade through a great pile of academic decisions. So you're not alone. Scores of students have gone before you and survived. Finally, no matter what the academic caliber your school is thought to have, the quality of your education stems in large part from your own initiative and follow-through.

Details are unglamorous and often frustrating, but they always carry special importance. In the project of full-time academics, there is no shortage of decisions, dilemmas, and details. How many classes should I take? How do I decide which ones to take first? Which professors are the best? How do I use my academic advisor? Is it normal to be spending this much money on textbooks? To help you face these many issues, we'd like to give you a few points of simple age-old wisdom to take into college right from the very beginning.

1. *Start by determining which classes you need to take.* Most colleges have some form of core curriculum that compels freshmen and sophomores to take courses in various disciplines. Learn what these general requirements consist of and map out how to fulfill them sooner rather than later. Implicit in this advice is the need to make sure you take all the required courses necessary for graduation. You'd be surprised how many seniors end up in lower-level language classes because they forgot to take them early on!

2. *Consider what classes you would like to take.* Skim over the course description manual and see what catches your eye. This is the fun part and a great perk of college life. Even the PE classes can be a wonderful break from the normal academic routine. Music, art, and photography are also popular categories to explore. Not every course is always available, but it

doesn't hurt to make a wish list to work from during the semesters ahead.

3. *Listen to your elders.* Older students know how the system works and have a well-seasoned feel for the options. Consult with them. Find out what they know about certain classes and professors. They may save you from a terrible experience or tell you about a great class you hadn't otherwise considered.

4. *Take classes with friends.* If there is a common interest in a class, by all means take advantage of it. Going to class with a friend or two makes it that much more exciting. I took several classes with one of my roommates, and we had a great time. Not only did it make preparing for exams easier when we could study together, we were also able to share and compare notes when needed.

5. *Remember that the professor makes or breaks the class.* When choosing classes it is easy to get drawn in by an exciting title or a subject that really interests you. Be careful! This is no guarantee that the class will actually be good. The quality of the professor matters more than the appeal of the subject. When it comes to required courses this can be difficult, even impossible when only one professor teaches the course. But when it comes to elective classes, nine times out of ten we recommend choosing the course based on who is teaching it. I once took an economics class (a subject I dislike) solely because of the professor and his teaching style. It was one of my best classes at college!

6. *Don't ever take a class because it is a guaranteed "easy A."* First of all, if you're taking a class just so you can get a good grade without any work, your attitude is all wrong. Second, you should be forewarned that classes like this almost always require more work than you expect, and rarely get you an A. I took several of these and always ended up with Bs.

7. *Be reasonable.* Many a well-intentioned student starts the semester full of motivation and later learns that six honors classes is too much to handle. As a basic rule we suggest taking no more than fifteen credit hours—usually five classes—and avoiding schedules where every class requires huge loads

of reading and writing. Make things doable; there's no reason to overburden yourself.

8. *Plan to graduate on time.* It's true that good reasons can compel some students to opt for the five-year plan, but this is a decision best left for later on. Keep in mind the question of stewardship.

If you have done your best to follow these guidelines in choosing classes and still find that after two weeks into classes you think you've made a mistake—fear not. Most schools offer some kind of drop-add period in which they allow you to scout out your classes and make adjustments if need be. While it's not a good idea to rely on this grace period, it can be a great way out of a jam early on.

Because professors are so central to your education, once the semester is off and running, it is time to take some initiative in getting to know them. The idea here is not to get ahead or win their favor but to take them seriously as people and make a point of building relationships of trust and respect with them. If, after all, you are to be learning from them and treating them as the Bereans treated Paul and his teaching, it helps to know them and build trust so that you can speak freely with them. Every professor is required to hold office hours where he or she is accessible to students. Take advantage of these. Ask follow-up questions about their last lecture, find out what suggestions they have for getting all you can from the course. If they seem open to talking further, try to meet them for coffee or hot chocolate (if you're like John). Most professors appreciate this kind of interaction and respond to it well. Moreover, many schools actually have funds available to students just for these purposes!

Decidedly Undecided

Wedged somewhere between the questions "Where do you go to college?" and "Do you know my second cousin? she goes there too" in any standard introduction these days is always the unfailing query "What's your major?" Your parents, your friends, and even your parents' friends are all waiting anxiously to see what your decision is. Amid a whole collection of life-changing priorities and responsibilities during the college years, our *major* is a major part of our identity.

So why all the fuss? The short answer is that our majors are, after all, the central focus of our academic experience. They are our specialty, our area of expertise and concentration. If being a student is a nine-to-five occupation, the major is treated as the main task in your job description. But must it be such a big priority? The obvious answer to this is, yes, of course it matters. However, it's a priority that needs to be kept in balance. Deciding what to major in need not be the most terrible and painstaking decision of college life. That said, it's still a decision, and we want to take a quick look at a few common approaches students take to making it.

In the first group are those students who decide their major according to very practical and long-term purposes. For example, they know they want to go to graduate school or work in a particular field such as business or medicine, so they choose that same field for their undergraduate work. It works well for some students, but it's not always necessary. Very few students actually follow this course during their four years. Many start by selecting a major for reasons such as these but end up changing several times.

The second group of students are those who major in the thing they love. Patrick loves political science, so he makes it his major. Jaime realizes she keeps enrolling in British literature courses, so hey, why not major in it? This is kind of the no-brainer approach—not that it's stupid, just practical in a different way. Instead of the pressure of "What *should* I major in?" it's the calm decision of "What do I *want* to spend my time studying? What do I enjoy?" Can groups one and two overlap? Yes, and that is often an ideal situation, one which we'll come back to in just a minute.

The final group of students includes those who major in something for reasons they can't remember. It's surprising how many people fall into this category. "Why am I majoring in sociology? I hate sociology!" Many times this occurs because students select a major their freshman year that they think they love, only to realize a year or two down the road that they're sick of it. We don't recommend being in this group.

During my freshman and sophomore years I changed my major a total of four times. After losing faith in my ability to be major-committed, I latched on to the wonderful liberty of claiming "undecided" as my temporary answer. I soon realized most of the classes I was taking were in American history, which I really enjoyed as a subject. At last, a major to stick with! After I became peaceful with the undecided label, things began to work themselves out. For this reason, many students suggest that, if possible, decide to be undecided. In other words, don't make the formal decision before it needs to be made. At most colleges students do not have to officially declare their major until the end of sophomore year. This means there's some time to relax and think about it.

So how do you make a good decision? We mentioned above that the ideal situation for choosing a major is one in which you choose it for long-term practical career purposes and at the same time simply for the love of the subject. This won't happen to everyone, but it could happen more often. It just takes a little bit of thought.

When choosing a major, you don't necessarily need to know what you want to do with the rest of your life. It helps to know, but this is often unrealistic. What we advocate, instead, is exploring your sense of calling in a more general way by starting with the question "What am I good at?" God gives each of us special gifts and abilities. My friend Bryan wanted to be a doctor. So right from the beginning of college he started taking premed classes. The problem was that he wasn't all that great at chemistry and biology, the two big premed classes. After almost two years of suffering, Bryan decided to change direction. He ended up majoring in religious studies, which he was good at, and taking a lot of classes in the business school, which he was also good at. Now he is a successful financial planner and is also active in bringing his gifts and skills into involvement at his local church. Like Bryan, your gifts and abilities will help direct you to what you should be studying. Most likely you're good at certain subjects and not so good at others. It's pretty basic, but being honest with yourself and simply gauging your abilities helps go a long way toward figuring out what to major in.

Alongside this process of determining what you're good at is the important process of figuring out what you enjoy. God doesn't call us into professions we hate just to torment us. Instead, he has a way of giving us a love for things we are good at and calling us into them. *It is when your gifts and abilities coincide with your likes and interests that you have discovered what subject to major in.*

Sometimes we love things and end up being terrible at them. And sometimes we don't enjoy what we're good at. Don't take these situations as defeat; take them as a signal to keep thinking and exploring your options. Bryan loves being a financial planner, and although he is still interested in medicine, he knows how much happier he is doing what he's doing. It was hard for him to give up something he loved, but he trusted God in the process and soon discovered another subject that he enjoyed and that helped prepare him for his future job.

Is one major more Christian than another? Shouldn't I major in religious studies and not finance? Is it possible for God to be glorified in an engineering degree? We hope the answers to these questions are obvious. Just as no career is more godly than another, no major is more Christian than another. For our godliness is determined not so much by what we are doing but by how we go about doing it. If the Lord has given us a passion and skills for certain subject areas, we should go after them, treating our academic lives as a matter of stewardship of God's gifts to us.

Overdoing It?

One of the great ironies of college life is that those students who *really* do make academics a priority are often thought to be overdoing it. We all have different expectations that go along with assumptions we make about what being a student should look like. I might assume three hours of studying a day is enough for anyone, but my hardworking friend might expect to hit the books for more like five hours each day (including Saturdays). There are as many *methods* to managing student life as there are *priorities* in living it. And how we manage our time and academic energy is a matter of how we set and keep those priorities. Sometimes priorities present challenges.

What happens when academics and relationships come into conflict? How do we balance our priorities? How do we deal with all the different pressures on us at school and still succeed academically?

Michael knew all along that he wanted to go to medical school, and one of the best, at that. As a result, he consciously decided to put academics above all but his closest relationships and most important responsibilities. During the course of his college career, a few people ended up getting hurt because they felt Michael had his priorities mixed up. They couldn't understand why he was always studying and rarely had time for them. Michael knows he sometimes shut people out, and recognizes this was unfortunate, but has no regrets today. He realized that his primary ministry was to be the best premed student he could be, so that he could be a good medical student and prepare to become the best doctor he could be. He is now finishing his final year at arguably the best medical school in the world. He will, without a doubt, be a stellar doctor. Thank goodness he was a wise steward of his academic gifts.

In contrast to Michael, I tended to put relationships right up there with academics in my priorities. I don't regret this, but I realize that my academics weren't as strong as they could have been as a result. It was a conscious decision, like Michael's, that I don't regret, but it had its costs. I knew all through college that I was ultimately going to go into some kind of full-time work in church ministry. Because of this I knew that lessons I could learn about ministry and relationships were of central importance to my overall education at college. Thankfully, I had many opportunities to learn and grow in relational ministry. Now I'm in graduate school working on a degree in theology. This year my focus is academic, and I'm finding it necessary to place most relationships farther down the ladder of my priorities. This is tough, but my stewardship of this graduate degree depends on putting academics at the top.

Different times in life, different gifts, different callings all go into showing us what our academic priorities should be, remembering all along that our full-time occupation at college is that of a student. The important lesson to learn for setting these kinds of priorities is that any decision of this nature has to be conscious—academics don't just happen; they should be given a specific priority. The second lesson is learning to communicate your priorities to your friends so that they understand you and can help you meet your goals. The third lesson is to realize that giving certain things high priority means other things will suffer. Because you can't do everything, be willing to sacrifice some things to become a good steward of others.

Adventures Abroad?

You're in your sophomore year, perhaps studying a foreign language that you love or taking lots of classes in English literature. One Tuesday morning your professor hands out information sheets about studying abroad during your junior year. Hmm. You've never really thought about it before, but it could be fun.

To study abroad, or not to study abroad? That is the question. For some of us this will never be an option or a desire, but for others considering this opportunity, there are a number of things to think about before signing on the dotted line and converting your parents' money into some foreign currency.

For many, the study-abroad decision is a terribly complicated and agonizing one. Not to mention the task of convincing the parents it's a good idea. While it certainly is an important decision, we come from the perspective that it should be kept as uncomplicated as possible. Students who spent semesters studying abroad conveyed to us several basic considerations helpful to think about in considering the idea. As you'll see, the possibilities for both pros and cons tend to go hand in hand.

First, being in another country can provide a wonderful new perspective on the world, on life, and on the American culture you left behind. *But* it can also be lonely and will require some tough adjustments. Second, time abroad can be a great getaway from the normal routine of your campus back home. *But* it's easy to miss the old way of life on campus when everything around you is forcing you into a new routine, and usually a new language. Third, think of all the cool new people you will meet! *But* leaving your normal college world means leaving your relationships and other commitments there on hold. Many students who study abroad have a tough time getting back into the close friendships they left behind—even if e-mail is available overseas, it's not the same as being around each other day in and day out.

All this is to say that it's an option we need to be realistic about. For some, studying abroad is an amazing time of perspective-building and spiritual growth. The Lord will certainly use the challenges of it to draw you into greater reliance on him. For others, unrealistic expectations pave the way for a disappointing time and a tough reentry back on campus. A lot of prayer, some consideration of needs and goals, and careful research into different programs will generally make the study-abroad question mark a lot less agonizing. So explore the options, weigh the pros and cons, and let the Lord lead you to the right decision at the right time.

Navigating through the pushing and pulling currents of academic life is a challenge. We are tossed about by all the decisions and dilemmas we face in choosing classes, professors, majors, and so on. These all call for our attention and management, and many times we simply have to learn as we go. But it's a good journey and an adventure that asks for our best efforts. By looking at being a student as a *calling,* we see that it is far more than a mere experience of getting by. Our discernment and effort are being called into service. By responding with initiative, we see that we can bring our Christian minds into full-time action.

Questions for Study and Reflection

Study passages: Micah 6:8; Colossians 3:23–24

1. What are some of your academic goals for college? What does it mean to be called to be a student?

2. Do you follow a full-time framework in your approach to being a student? If not, what needs to change to make you a full-time student?

3. What do you or might you enjoy studying? What areas are you best at? Do the two lists overlap anywhere? If so, might that be a good consideration for a possible major?

4. What are the leading distractions keeping you from pouring yourself into your academic life? What can be done to get around them?

5. Make a list of the advantages and disadvantages of studying abroad. Even if you've never considered it before, could this be something for you?

CONFLICT ON CAMPUS

CHAPTER 16

Life on a college campus is like a television miniseries in some ways. Take all the drama, tension, and trouble in life and pack it into a set of episodes featuring a cast of opinionated and potentially irritating people. Good conflict, after all, makes for good drama. Campus life may lack the Hollywood commercial appeal, but conflict is often the daily story line. When you bring together all kinds of people from all sorts of backgrounds with a wide variety of opinions about life, things can get a little tense. Consider these actual headlines from student newspapers reflecting some of the issues and debates that arise during the course of college life:

Campus Political Groups Debate Views of Abortion
"Gendered Language" Must Go
Student Congress Votes to Fund Minority Recruitment
Pot-Smoking Incident a Cry for Help
Making Friends of Other Race Not Hard When Proud of Self
Human Cloning Prompts Moral, Scientific Questions
Diverse Thoughts on Spiritual Expression
Just Talk to Someone, Anyone, about Depression

Time to Search for Your Own Definition of Life
Rally to Support Diversity
Don't Accept Predefined Happiness: Find Own Joy
Who Deserves Capital Punishment in America?
Students Promote Abstinence through New Group
Police Determine Recent Assault to Be Rape
Christians, Put Your Eyes Back in Your Reason
"Sodomy" Stigmatizes Fun, Liberating Sexual Acts

Though just a sampling, these headlines are enough to make our heads swim. Conflict on campus comes in many forms: through social issues, relationships, student groups, class readings, lectures, over lunch, at student meetings . . . and on and on and on. Conflict doesn't occur because "all your professors will be communists!" or because "everyone's a crazy liberal!" as you may have been warned. Conflict occurs because the college campus has a way of breathing a spirited life into tough questions about fundamental values. It's a real-life drama unfolding every day, and it's important that we as Christians know how to handle it.

Beware the Yeast . . .

In Matthew 16, we find Jesus traveling with the disciples across a lake. He had just come from another frustrating encounter with the Pharisees and Sadducees, skeptical Jewish teachers and politicians who loved to argue with Jesus, even though they always lost. Fresh from this encounter, Jesus warns the disciples in verse 6, "Be careful. . . . Be on your guard against the *yeast* of the Pharisees and Sadducees." Confused, the disciples think he's talking about bread but can't quite figure out why. Jesus goes on to explain, and at last they get it: he is warning them about the *teachings* of the Pharisees and Sadducees.

But what does yeast have to do with teaching? According to *The American Heritage Dictionary*, yeast, chemically speaking, is an "agent of ferment or activity." It is a key ingredient for making bread and wine, among other things. And it is very complex—so complex that scientists are amazed by it. Not long ago we came across the following report: "A worldwide collaboration of more than one hundred laboratories has accomplished a significant first in scientific research, the sequencing of the complete genome of a complex organism . . . baker's yeast. The achievement marks the complete sequencing of the largest genome to date—more than twelve million base pairs of DNA. . . . The biggest surprise was that more than half of the six thousand genes uncovered during the sequencing were unknown, despite decades of intense scrutiny" (Sean Henahan, "Complete DNA Sequence of Yeast," *Access Excellence,* 24 April 1996). It's probably a safe guess to say that the disciples didn't know this at the time.

For the disciples, yeast was a simple household ingredient. In their day grocery stores weren't exactly on every corner. If you wanted bread, you knew how to bake it—and you knew the importance of yeast. You would be surprised at the small amount of yeast actually used in making bread. A tiny bit of yeast causes bread dough to rise in dramatic ways. What Jesus was conveying to the disciples was that the teaching of the Pharisees and Sadducees worked in a similar way. Their skewed thinking could work its way into people's minds in small quantities and begin to rise into dangerous ideas opposed to Jesus' message. Because yeast comes in small amounts, you often don't see it thrown into the dough and don't notice it until the dough begins to rise. When it came to false teaching, this was dangerous and required that the disciples be extra alert and sensitive to even the slightest falsehoods.

Jesus' warning still stands for Christians in today's world. We don't exactly have Pharisees and Sadducees to deal with, but there are many other teachers and skeptics inserting falsehoods into the way people think. College campuses are breeding grounds for these bad ideas. There are messages from professors, friends, student interest groups, books, newspapers . . . the list goes on. It's nearly impossible to pay close attention to everything and even tougher to take steps to filter out the good from the bad. This is why we so strongly emphasized in chapter 14 the need to filter everything through God's Word. "Beware the yeast" is a warning we need to take seriously. What does modern-day yeast look like? What are we to watch for? How do we deal with it when we find it?

Conflict in the Classroom

I once took a European politics seminar taught by a kind, soft-spoken, and intriguing Swiss man who was a very popular professor on campus. Each week, twenty of us would gather around a large table for discussion on a variety of topics—generally having little or nothing to do with political science. Professor Fritz would introduce a topic by posing a question or sharing a story, and then we would find ourselves stewing over what was, at heart, a matter of ideology or belief. Often we wrestled with tough questions that reached beyond the classroom and into our lives. And boy, did we disagree a lot.

In the class session following our midterm exam Professor Fritz walked in with a stack of exams under his arm. As he sat down in front of us at the head of the discussion table he said, "I want to know if you believe there is a fair way in which these tests can be graded." Huh? Not exactly what one expects to hear from a professor. "What I mean is, do you believe there are really *objective* standards for grading, or is my perspective somehow biased because of what *I* believe to be true?" He had, indeed, graded the exams, but he wanted to use the process of grading to illustrate a deeper question: "Am I really capable of being a fair judge?" Essentially, the question this brilliant political scientist was getting at was *"Who am I to say that what you wrote is true or false?"*

One hears this kind of statement expressed in different ways all across today's college campuses. "I can't speak for everyone, but what *I* believe is . . ."; "That may be *true for you,* but it's not for me." The prevailing belief is that no one can say what is true, wrong, or right for other people. In a nutshell, truth is *relative.* Given our understanding of truth discussed in chapter 14, this point poses problems for the Christian. As Professor Fritz asked his question, I remember thinking, "Here we go . . . my faith is about to get ridiculed." I knew that a conflict was brewing in my classroom—a conflict between popularly accepted secular views and less-popular Christian beliefs.

If, after all, each of us is capable of determining for ourselves what is right and wrong, true and false, then who am I to disagree? One student claimed, "There really are no objective criterion or truths—no truths that are in themselves *true,* apart from man's interpretation." A student across the room responded, "Ideally I'm a relativist—I'll accept everything people believe—but clearly we need some rules." What an odd statement! How could he affirm relativism (a virtual free-for-all of ideas and beliefs) and then at the same time admit a need for rules?

The discussion soon turned to matters of religion, and I felt the tension increase. Because all the religions in the world simply can't be true at the same time, it made for a good point of discussion. Professor Fritz, in his usual honesty, said, "I stopped going to church after I was young, and I do not believe there is *one* true religion. However, I do believe there is something higher, and it is the fate of human beings that *we don't know* what that thing is. Life is a constant search for it." It was a painful statement, and while I disagreed with his view, I felt a lot of hurt for him. In grading our exams, he was evaluating our answers according to a standard that he as the expert knew better than any of us. He had to say there was a *right* and a *wrong* in terms of the course material. In matters of faith, however, he was settling for a relativist view of truth and succumbing to the popular idea that there is no ultimate Truth.

My experiences in class that day revealed two varieties of yeast that Christians are likely to come up against. First, the yeast of *relativism* causes many people to assume that truth is up to each person and absolutes can't possibly exist. A *diversity* of opinions about truth is preferred over any strict claims about Truth. Second, when it comes to matters of faith especially, there is a general unwillingness to say anything that would be divisive or that would call someone else's belief wrong. Instead, the general consensus is to be *tolerant* of all faith claims and lifestyles *except* Christianity, which is said to be intolerant of other views. Tolerance is the aggressive *acceptance* of all viewpoints and lifestyles as equally true and good. Diversity is the *celebration* of these differences. Together they forge a commitment to not offending as the noblest of goals. If you find something offensive and wrong, you are close-minded. If you offend someone with your own views, you're from the dark ages.

It was interesting that I was not *attacked* outright that day for being a Christian, but it was certainly *implied* that my Christian "god" could in no way compare to these classroom gods of tolerance and diversity. Direct attacks on our faith (and how it colors our viewpoint) do occur, but conflict in the classroom does not always feel intense. Instead, classroom opinions and arguments have a subtle way of making it seem that our faith is outdated, mindless, and intolerant and shouldn't be taken seriously. What we eventually realize we're up against, at secular colleges especially, is a totally different way of looking at the world. The fundamental principles we as Christians have about God, man, and society—the core truths of what might be called our *worldview*—are not shared.

To try and dig up all the thorny roots of campus issues and colliding worldviews in any depth requires a full-length book. Many very good books dealing with these questions have been written and are out there for us to consult (see those included in our suggested reading list). These books discuss the detailed makeup of our Christian worldview in contrast to commonly held beliefs and are definitely worth delving into. Because there are so many good resources, we don't want to go over the same ground here. In the rest of this chapter our desire is to construct a framework for dealing with ideological conflict and to encourage a specific mindset as we engage with others. First, we'll take a look at what it means to be a *subversive Christian* doing strategic work in the world. Then we want to encourage all believers to develop an *apologetic of integrity*. By *apologetic* we mean a way of explaining and defending the faith as we live it out. With these interrelated strategies we are able to enter the fray with a focus on Christ as lord and with the attitude of servants.

Subversive Christianity

Is there a way to counteract the effects of yeast? A way to neutralize the influence of false ideas and misguided ideals that creep across campus and into our classrooms? Yes, there is a way, and it just so happens to be summed up in the effects of another ingredient sometimes used in making bread: salt. If the teaching of the Pharisees and Sadducees was like yeast, then the teaching of Jesus and the apostles was to be like salt. In his Sermon on the Mount Jesus challenged his listeners, saying, "You are the salt of the earth." What does he mean by this?

It could be said that salt has two major characteristics. It both *penetrates* and *preserves*. Salt is often used to add flavor to a dish. In this sense it penetrates whatever it is we are cooking and adds a great deal to the final dish. Although salt is most often used as a seasoning nowadays, it was frequently used as a preservative in Jesus' day. Fish and other meats would have been salted and stored in a cellar for future use. Without salt it would have all gone bad. In this way salt acted to preserve the goodness of the meat until it was ready for consumption.

In the same way, if we are to be the salt of the earth, we should seek both to penetrate the world around us with the truth of the gospel and to preserve what redemptive features do remain in it. *Another way to look at it is that we should seek to subvert (that is, to overturn) what is false and uphold what is true.* In this sense we should think of ourselves as subversive Christians. Sounds kind of fun, doesn't it?

To Penetrate

What does it look like to penetrate an idea with the gospel, exposing its falsehood, and also to preserve what is good about it? Let's take a closer look at those gods of the ivory tower, tolerance and diversity, and see what we can discover.

We start by unpacking the shallowness of these ideals and penetrating them with the profound truth of the gospel. If a belief system is built on tolerance and diversity as its guiding principles, it is built without any concrete claims to truth. Instead of drawing conclusions about the world from a specific source of truth, one simply accepts everything as true and draws any conceivable conclusion he desires. Ultimately this means believing in nothing. In this situation belief becomes a matter of preference and opinion instead of a matter of truth. With no permanent sense of truth in which to root one's life, one's identity exists in a state of constant flux. This may be fun for a few years of experimentation and exploration in college, but a lifetime without a concrete sense of personal identity is both meaningless and terrifying. Those whom the yeast has gotten hold of may not acknowledge this, but they will likely have some sense of the perpetual emptiness that comes from believing in everything and thus believing in nothing.

This is, we realize, not an exhaustive look at what's wrong with tolerance and diversity, but it serves to give at least some idea of what we mean by penetrating falsehood with truth. Your fellow students need to be led to see these things. By showing the shortcomings of campus ideologies, we prepare the way for the fullness and depth of Christian truth. This takes patience, well-worded points, and often creativity. The gospel teaches us a truth that is timeless and at the same time historical in that it descended to earth in Christ. This is radical. The Christian actually *believes* in something. We build our lives on the truth of our redemption. Because of this we know that a life without foundation is not only miserable, it is false. In this simple and straightforward way, we see that the gospel may penetrate and gain a foothold against the yeast. At the same time, it is crucial to take on the second quality of salt as we look to preserve what, if anything, might be redeemable.

To Preserve

How *do* Christians think about tolerance? Even poor ideologies often start with good intentions and some notion of truth. Is there any common ground or meaningful starting point with tolerance? While we don't worship tolerance, we do proclaim a gospel of unconditional love. This is a helpful starting point. The gospel of Christ is a message for everyone—it doesn't discriminate. It begins by saying that all people are equal before God—no one is better off than anyone else regardless of how good a person you may be. We are *all* sinful and *all* fall short of God's glory (Rom. 3:23). Not only are we equally fallen and separated from God, we are all given the opportunity for redemption through Christ. Jesus didn't die just for the Jews or just for people who do good works; he died for everyone. The gospel of Jesus is open to all people because all of us are equally separated from God and because Jesus died for us all.

When looked at in this way, we see that the gospel addresses those deeper needs lurking behind the modern ideal of tolerance: a need to be loved for who we are and a need to be treated with the same dignity and respect as everyone else. Christians cannot approve of every claim to truth and every lifestyle, but we can love people. We can respectfully disagree. And we can share a gospel that has no tolerance for sin whatsoever but reveals a love intended for everyone without discrimination. Who, having the option, would choose to be tolerated over being loved?

How *can* Christians celebrate diversity? This one is easy: God created diversity. Diversity for its own sake is nothing to get excited about—it's merely colorful—but diversity that is a demonstration of the character of God is something much more exciting. Our diversity becomes meaningful only when it is anchored in God, reflecting both the creativity of God and the nature of God. God is trinity: Father, Son, and Holy Spirit. As a trinity, God is diverse; he is a community unto himself. Thus our tremendous diversity as human beings reflects some of this diversity within God himself. It also reflects God's massive creativity. As we look around us even at the simple physical differences between people, we catch a glimpse of the limitlessness of God's creative power. When seen in the light of the truth of the gospel, diversity is a wonderful feature of our human existence, something that leads us into worship of an amazing God.

Subversive Christians have a strategy. We are able to see the false gods worshiped around us, and through discussion and debate we penetrate them with the truth of the gospel. Subversive Christians are also able to lift what is good out of the bad—to dig in and find the redeemable elements mixed in with the false ones. In this way we preserve what is already good while allowing what is false to be destroyed in the face of the gospel. A subversive Christian is a salty Christian.

After telling his followers to be the salt of the earth, Jesus goes on to say in Matthew 5:13, "But if the salt loses its saltiness, how can it be made salty again? It is no longer good for anything, except to be thrown out and trampled by men." Ouch. This sounds pretty harsh. We are given two choices: either be salt or be trampled. If we aren't actively being the salt of the earth, we will get trampled by other people. If we aren't actively seeking to be subversive Christians, we aren't much use at all, and the prevailing culture on campus will walk all over us.

The Apologetic of Integrity: Proclaiming Truth, Explaining Truth, and Living It Out

During his final year of college Andy was in a small seminar studying contemporary American culture. Ashley, a lesbian girl with whom he had shared several classes, was also in the seminar. One afternoon the discussion was devoted to gay issues. Predictably, things quickly heated up. Everyone in the class, except Ashley, was straight, and they began to get a little carried away in their condemnation of gay lifestyles. What began as a discussion about gay issues quickly turned into a gay-bashing session during which Ashley was left to the mercy of her classmates. They weren't very nice. After having enough, Andy stepped in. "You all know that I think homosexuality is wrong and that in all honesty I find it pretty repulsive," he said, "but homosexuality is a real issue, and these are real people we're talking about— let's be sensitive to that." As a Christian, and one whom everyone knew had strong feelings against homosexuality, Andy's simple comment had the affect of completely hushing the conversation. Ashley was left alone and her classmates sheepishly refocused.

After class Ashley went up to Andy with tears in her eyes. "You know that I disagree with you on just about everything, and I know that you think my lifestyle is wrong," she said and then paused before saying, "I don't know how to describe exactly how I feel right now, except to say that I feel cherished by you." Wow. Having kept quiet for most of class, Andy had stepped in and with a few simple words completely changed the tone of the discussion. He showed someone in a dramatic way the love of Christ.

Three years later Andy and Ashley are still in touch. She has started going to a church and is beginning to leave her lesbian lifestyle. Undoubtedly this is the work of God, but you know that it had something to do with Andy being a faithful witness who at the right time said a few thoughtful words and stuck his neck out for someone just because he loved her.

Discussions involving the big issues in life can get nasty sometimes. How might you have responded to Ashley during class? While it is true that in many situations non-Christians get carried away in their exasperation with the "narrow-minded" views of Christians, Christians are often quick to be defensive and arrogant. The temptation is for us to think we need to be soldiers for the truth going out to do *battle*. After the battle is done, what has been accomplished? Discussions end and people go their separate ways, shaking their heads at how narrow and unreceptive everyone else is. Nothing is gained except more wounds that will become scars. This is the way of the world; it happens through two basic methods: *argument*, not discussion, and *insisting* instead of listening. Anger is more prevalent than trust. The problem in these situations is that the practice of defending ideologies has taken place at the expense of maintaining relationships. Relationships eventually disintegrate as a result, leaving no room for more meaningful interaction down the road. This is likely to have happened between the class's other students and Ashley.

As Christians we must be careful not to borrow the world's strategies. When we disagree with someone, it must not keep us from loving them. If we want to be heard, we must win trust. Without affirming her lifestyle and without being tolerant in the way we're encouraged to be by the secular sensitivity police, Andy showed Ashley that he loved her and that she was valued as a person regardless of their disagreements. This is what the apologetic of integrity looks like. It involves consistently proclaiming the truth, even when it is unpopular. It involves explaining the truth, even when people might not be listening. And finally, it means living out that truth in every situation, that people might see the principles of lordship, integrity, and servanthood in action.

During her second year at a small liberal arts college in the Northwest, Trina enrolled in a women's studies seminar. Knowing very little about women's studies, Trina was curious and hoped the seminar would prove to be a good introduction to cool ways of thinking about women, the family, and society. From the first day of class it was all too obvious things were not as Trina had hoped. She was introduced to new ways of thinking, but they were far from the introduction she had anticipated. "The spirit of the class and everything that was taught seemed to go against my own beliefs," she said. "It was a harsh feminist ideology that was pro-choice and anti-men. I felt so out of place and intimidated. These weren't my views, and I didn't know how to respond." Up against these obvious challenges, Trina decided to stick it out and stayed involved in the class. Though the views of the other students and the claims of the professor cut against her core beliefs, she made a point of listening carefully to everyone. "I almost never said anything; I just listened and tried to build a sense of trust with the other students."

One day the discussion was centered on abortion, and Trina felt that if there was one issue she had to speak out on, it was this one. "Everyone was totally in favor of abortion without giving any thought to the other side. This made my stomach turn. I was scared to speak up, but I felt like I had to." Her decision paid off. While she had been listening to her fellow classmates for most of the semester, she was now given the floor to speak. For about five minutes she patiently and carefully explained her views on the subject and how they were based on the deeper principles of her faith. Her classmates listened. She may not have changed any minds, but she won some listeners. Though she had almost nothing in common with the class, Trina had earned the right to make a stand. As a result of her ability to listen, she also ended up developing a good relationship with the professor, and though they disagreed on pretty much everything, the professor later wrote a strong letter of recommendation on Trina's behalf.

Once again we see the apologetic of integrity at work. Trina demonstrated her care for those around her by *respecting* them and *listening* to their side of the story. When the time was right she stood up for what she believed, knowing that it was contradictory to the prevailing opinion of the class. She proclaimed truth, she explained truth, and she lived it out convincingly by having enough confidence in it to listen to other people and respect them in spite of their misguided views.

We must care passionately about the things we believe in. It is unquestionable that ideas matter, and we must never compromise in what we believe to be true. Alongside this, and as a part of this, we must value relationships, for relationships are at the heart of the gospel. Our faith is not limited to our intellect but is something that spills over into all facets of life. Faith is a relationship we share rather than simply a set of ideas we seek to impose. As a result we place a high value on our relationships with people. We don't do this at the expense of truth; on the contrary, we do it that truth might be more *fully* proclaimed. What the Christian must do is learn to disagree and debate in such a way that proclaims the truth while showing the overpowering presence of Christ. Tough? Sure. Impossible? Not with the power of the Holy Spirit.

Think about Andy and Ashley. Ashley knew exactly what Andy thought about homosexuality because he had never hidden his beliefs or refused to justify them. He was faithful to the truth of Scripture as it relates to sexuality (Andy was a good Berean!). In addition to this Andy was also faithful to the truth of the gospel that says we are all precious in the eyes of Christ, that he died for every last one of us. Just as Jesus went out of his way to love those whom society had said were unlovable, so Andy loved Ashley.

Truth needs ambassadors, not soldiers. People willing to proclaim it, explain it, and live it out. This is the profound challenge and amazing opportunity that awaits us at college.

Christ Crucified

When we seek to develop an apologetic of integrity, our greatest strength as apologists is the same as the apostle Paul's. In his first letter to the Corinthians he puts it so well: "Where is the wise man? Where is the scholar? Where is the philosopher of this age? Has not God made foolish the wisdom of the world? For since in the wisdom of God the world through its wisdom did not know him, God was pleased through the foolishness of what was preached to save those who believe. Jews demand miraculous signs and Greeks look for wisdom, but we preach Christ crucified. . . .

For the foolishness of God is wiser than man's wisdom, and the weakness of God is stronger than man's strength."

Paul continues a paragraph later, saying, "When I came to you, brothers, I did not come with eloquence or superior wisdom as I proclaimed to you the testimony about God. For I resolved to know nothing while I was with you except Jesus Christ and him crucified. I came to you in weakness and fear, and with much trembling. My message and my preaching were not with wise and persuasive words, but with a demonstration of the Spirit's power, so that your faith might not rest on men's wisdom, but on God's power" (1 Cor. 1:20–23, 25; 2:1–5).

Isn't it a wonderful relief to see that Paul, the greatest apologist for the faith of all time, was weak and scared at times? He knew both the absurdity and the power of preaching Christ crucified. He also knew the way in which the Spirit is able to work in people's lives. Although Paul was a crafty debater and skilled rhetorician, he clung to the conviction that the foundational truth of Christ's death and resurrection was what needed to be proclaimed. He knew that the ultimate power that accomplished this was the Holy Spirit. We need to keep the same things in mind as we engage with those around us. For all the principles that lay beneath the tides and currents of ideological conflict on campus must ultimately reckon with the truth of Christ crucified.

Classroom debate, after-class discussions, and late-night conversations in the dorm can help lead people to question their underlying assumptions about the way the world works. In all of these situations we must be mindful of our role as ambassadors of Christ. We are not simply students with Christian outlooks and opinions. We are Christ's representatives and need to present him faithfully to those around us. For it is Christ alone, through the power of the Holy Spirit, who radically gets hold of a person's heart and mind and clears out the yeast that has crept in and corrupted his or her perspective. Our role in this process will sometimes be as basic as sharing a well-thought-through perspective on a political issue or at other times artfully subverting common assumptions about the world. Far more often, however, it will mean living by faith in Christ in such a way that visibly and actively undermines the worldviews of others by demonstrating his lordship. How is this done? We like to think of this as an apologetic of integrity.

We proclaim truth, we explain truth, and we live out truth.

Questions for Study and Reflection

Study passage: Colossians 4:2–6

1. What is the most common form of yeast you come across in the way your friends think or in the way subjects are taught at school?

2. Right after Jesus challenges his followers to be the salt of the earth, he also tells them that they are the light of the world. What do you think this means? How are the two related?

3. What might it look like for you to be a subversive Christian on campus? Are there Christian friends who can share this vision with you?

4. In your own words, how would you describe what it means to have an apologetic of integrity? What role does prayer play in all of this?

5. What is the ultimate goal of having an apologetic of integrity? What is it that we want to communicate to those around us?

FOR FURTHER READING

Phyllis and James Alsdurf, *Eating Disorders* (InterVarsity Press, 1999).

Keith Anderson, *What They Don't Always Teach You at a Christian College* (InterVarsity Press, 1995).

Dietrich Bonhoeffer, *The Cost of Discipleship* (SCM Press Ltd., 1959).

Dietrich Bonhoeffer, *Life Together* (Harper and Row Publishers, Inc., 1954).

Jerry Bridges, *The Practice of Godliness* (NavPress, 1996).

Jerry Bridges, *The Pursuit of Holiness* (NavPress, 1978).

J. Budziszewski, *How to Stay Christian in College: An Interactive Guide to Keeping the Faith* (NavPress, 1999).

Robbie Castleman, *True Love in a World of False Hopes: Sex, Romance and Real People* (InterVarsity Press, 1996).

Robert Coleman, *The Master Plan of Evangelism* (Fleming H. Revell Co., 1993).

Richard Foster, *Celebration of Discipline* (Harper and Row Publishers, Inc., 1978).

Steve Garber, *The Fabric of Faithfulness* (InterVarsity Press, 1996).

C. S. Lewis, *Mere Christianity* (Macmillan Publishing Co., 1943).

George M. Marsden, *The Soul of the American University* (Oxford University Press, 1994).

Mark Noll, *The Scandal of the Evangelical Mind* (William B. Eerdmans Publishing Co., 1994).

J. I. Packer, *Evangelism and the Sovereignty of God* (InterVarsity Press, 1961).

J. I. Packer, *Knowing God* (InterVarsity Press, 1973).

John Perkins, *With Justice for All* (Regal Books, 1982).

Rebecca Manley Pippert, *Out of the Saltshaker and into the World: Evangelism as a Way of Life* (revised edition) (InterVarsity Press, 1999).

James W. Sire, *The Universe Next Door* (InterVarsity Press, 1988).

John Stott, *The Contemporary Christian* (InterVarsity Press, 1992).

John Stott, *Human Rights and Human Wrongs: Major Issues for a New Century,* volume 1 (Baker Book House, 1999).

John Stott, *Our Social and Sexual Revolution: Major Issues for a New Century*, volume 2 (Baker Book House, 1999).

John Stott, ed., *The Message of Acts: The Spirit, the Church, and the World* (InterVarsity Press, 1992). (We recommend any commentaries from *The Bible Speaks Today* series.)

John White, *Excellence in Leadership* (NavPress, 1999).

John White, *The Fight* (InterVarsity Press, 1976).

Albert Wolters, *Creation Regained: Biblical Basics for a Reformational Worldview* (William B. Eerdmans Publishing Co., 1985).

John Yates is a 1996 graduate of the University of Virginia where he helped lead a fellowship for first-year students, was involved in ministry with Young Life, and majored in religious studies. Having lived and studied in London for the past several years, John will begin seminary in the U.S. in the fall of 2000. **Chris Yates** is a 1998 graduate of the University of North Carolina at Chapel Hill where he wrote for the student newspaper, served in student government, and majored in history. He was involved with Campus Crusade for Christ and fellowship-based efforts toward Christian unity on campus.